D0835417

LANCA

Produced by the Salisbury Arts Theatre

Copyright (1958) by Peggy Simmons

Akin to Love

A Comedy in Three Acts

by PEGGY SIMMONS

CHARACTERS

(in the order of their appearance)

This comedy was first presented by Salisbury Arts Theatre Ltd. at the Salisbury Playhouse on August 11th, 1958, with the following cast:—

FLORRIE	Helen Dorward
ELIZABETH ALLEN, *the younger daughter*	... Ann Patrick
BERTHA TODD	Noreen Craven
TIMOTHY TODD, *Bertha's son*	... Ian Mullins
MAUD ALLEN...	Margaret Jones
TOM ALLEN	Geoffrey Lumsden
PRUDENCE BENNET, *the elder daughter*...	Cynthia Grenville
SALLY BENNET, *Prudence's daughter* ...	Mary Pat Morgan
EMMA JELLY	Jacqueline Boyer
REV. CHARLES FAIRFAX, *Bertha's nephew*	Timothy West

Directed by RONALD MAGILL

ACT I.   A morning in late July.

ACT II.   The same evening.

ACT III.   Morning a fortnight later.

THE SCENE throughout is the drawing room of the Allens' house in the village of Ashfield. There is a door R. and a french window back C. The fireplace is presumed to be in the " fourth wall," and facing it are chintz-covered armchairs R. and C. and a small sofa L. A table (large enough to hold the parcels in Act I) stands U.L. across the corner. A bookcase filled with books is R. of the window, and L. of the window is a standard lamp. One or two landscapes and family portraits decorate the walls, and the whole has an air of old-fashioned comfort.

Akin to Love

ACT I

A morning in late July.

(When the curtain goes up, ELIZABETH ALLEN, a woman in the late thirties, is arranging a pile of parcels on the small table U.L. She is neatly and sensibly dressed in the usual morning garb of the British housewife, not forgetting the apron, and holds a duster in her hand. A vacuum-cleaner and other evidences of the room being "done" are scattered about. A coat is slung over the back of the armchair C., and there are two books on the chair R. FLORRIE enters R. She looks about twenty-four, dressed in a rather lurid overall. She carries a greetings telegram envelope.)

FLORRIE   Telegram.

ELIZABETH   A telegram? Oh dear, what's happened now, I wonder.

FLORRIE   It's not the dangerous kind—only one of them fancy ones for your Mum and Dad. Many happy returns of their golden wedding, I should think, wouldn't you?

ELIZABETH   Oh, a greetings telegram. All right, thank you, Florrie. *(She comes towards FLORRIE, who takes no notice, but continues to examine the envelope for herself.)*

FLORRIE   My sister had one once for her birthday. It was ever so nice inside—bare babies and that all over it. Do you think we'd better open it to see if there's an answer? *(She turns the envelope over hopefully, almost as if to open it herself, but ELIZABETH takes it firmly from her.)*

ELIZABETH   There won't be an answer. I'll put it here with their other things. *Thank* you, Florrie. *(She returns to the table, and places the telegram on it.)*

FLORRIE *(ignoring the hint, and following ELIZABETH to the table)* Oh, haven't they got a nice lot of presents? Still, it's only right, after all. I mean, if you manage to be married for fifty years, you expect to see something for it, don't you? *(She examines a long narrow parcel)* I wonder what this one is? It feels like a cricket bat. But it wouldn't be, would it—not at their age.

ELIZABETH *(taking the parcel from FLORRIE, and putting it back on the table)* I shouldn't think so. Now, would you mind . . .

FLORRIE *(following ELIZABETH round as she dusts and tidies)* Still, you never know. People are funny, the things they think of. Someone gave my Grannie a pink nigh-long nightie when she

3

was eighty. She cut it off a bit, and used it as a slip, but she said there wasn't no real warmth in it. Old people do get some funny ideas.

ELIZABETH You're right—they do. Florrie, have you done the bathroom yet? *(She picks up the coat from chair C. and goes out R. with it , leaving the door open.* FLORRIE *follows her to the door and continues talking through it.)*

FLORRIE *(loudly)* No, I'm just going to. I couldn't, not before, because Mr. Allen got up so late. *(Half to herself, in a lower tone)* Nice mess it'll be in, too, as usual—water all over the floor, and shaving soap on the mirror. I don't know what he *does.* (ELIZABETH *re-enters R.)* Still, Mr. Allen's wonderful for his age, and you don't expect men to be like other people, do you?

ELIZABETH Florrie, I must get on. There's lots to do before the party tonight, and Miss Jelly'll be arriving very soon.

FLORRIE *(perching on the arm of the chair C.)* Miss Jelly—she was one of your Mum's bridesmaids, wasn't she? It's ever so nice, having the old bridesmaids to the golden wedding party. But two of them can't come, because they're dead, she told me. Pity, isn't it? Still, there's the Vicar's auntie as well, that makes two left. *(She takes a packet of cigarettes from her overall pocket.)*

ELIZABETH Florrie, if you mean Mrs. Todd, do say so, and don't always call her the Vicar's auntie. She doesn't like it.

FLORRIE Doesn't she? Well, she *is* the Vicar's auntie, and she lives with him and everything, so it comes more natural sort of. Everyone calls her that . . *(She lights a cigarette)* I can't see her as a bridesmaid, somehow. She doesn't look the type.

ELIZABETH That'll *do*, Florrie. Will you go and do the . . .

FLORRIE She's a bit of a tartar, if you don't mind me saying so. Well, I should know. I did for her last summer.

ELIZABETH You what?

FLORRIE Only for a few weeks, while Mrs. Wilkins had her leg. Mind you, the Vicar's ever so nice—not like a parson a bit—and so's Mr. Timothy when he's at home. But I don't care for the auntie myself. Now, I quite *like* working for you. Funny, isn't it?

ELIZABETH Yes, isn't it . . . I mean, look here, Florrie, you'll never get away by twelve if you don't get on.

FLORRIE I'm not in a hurry today—Kennie's having his dinner at school.

ELIZABETH *(U.R. at bookcase)* Oh . . . Well, I *am* in a hurry, so . . .

FLORRIE *(rising and going to* ELIZABETH*)* Always busy, aren't you? No wonder, with all you seem to have to do—looking after your Mum and Dad and everything else. It doesn't seem any sort of life to me. Tell you what, Miss Allen, you ought to have got married.

ELIZABETH Oh. Do you think so?

FLORRIE *(coming down C. again)* Well, of course, perhaps you never had the chance, or perhaps you didn't fancy it. But, by and large, everyone's better married, I always say.

ELIZABETH *(resignedly)* Well, you should know.

FLORRIE Me, Miss? . . . Oh, I see what you mean. We-ell, I generally call myself " Mrs.", because of Kennie, but I wouldn't say I wasn't open to a good offer . . . *(She drifts towards the door R.)* Oh, well, I mustn't let you keep me talking here, or I shan't get finished. I'm coming back tonight to help with the party. Shall I come a bit early, and help cut sandwiches and things?

ELIZABETH No, thank you very much, Florrie. I've got everything in hand—and we shan't need sandwiches.

FLORRIE Are you just having those little bits on biscuits, like Mrs. Wilkins said the Vicar's auntie did for her cocktail party? Mrs. Wilkins said there didn't look enough to feed a sparrow—no nourishment in any of it. I like a nice port or something myself, as well as anyone, but you do need something solid to . . . Well, talk of angels!

(BERTHA TODD, a battle-axe in the late sixties, comes in by the french window, followed by her son TIMOTHY, who is about 34. BERTHA carries a shopping basket full of parcels.)

BERTHA *(coming D.L. and putting the basket on the sofa)* Hullo, Elizabeth; thought we should find you here, so we came in this way. Good morning, Florrie. There's a telegraph boy at the door.

ELIZABETH *Another* telegram?

FLORRIE Oh, gracious me, no, it's the same one. I told him to wait for an answer. He said there wouldn't be, not with a greetings, but that's not your business, I said, better be safe than sorry. Then I got kept talking, and forgot about him. I say, aren't I awful? *(She rushes off R. with a scream of girlish laughter, leaving the door open.)*

BERTHA That girl's manners get worse and worse. I sometimes wonder if she's all there. ❧

ELIZABETH *(shutting the door after FLORRIE, and coming down R.)* Of course she's not all there. But she's the first one who hasn't given notice because of Mother, and I don't want to lose her. Any way, she's very good-natured, and she's quite a good worker when you can stop her talking.

BERTHA *Can* you stop her talking? *(She takes a shopping list from her bag, and begins to tick off the items, while ELIZABETH turns to TIMOTHY.)*

ELIZABETH No, I can't . . . Hello, Timothy, has your Select Seminary for Young Gentlemen broken up already?

TIMOTHY *(coming down C.)* The little devils were all disposed of yesterday morning, thank God, and I managed to get home last night. I hear you've got a party tonight. Can I come?

ELIZABETH Of course you can. Though I'm afraid it'll be a bit on the elderly side—it's Father's and Mother's golden wedding, you know. Mother wanted to make it a tea party, but it was Father who insisted on the cocktails, and for once he got his way. So there won't be many young ones, I'm afraid. Still, Sally's come down with Prudence, so she'll be there to amuse you.

TIMOTHY Sally always did amuse me. A rather grubby infant, if I remember rightly, but definitely fascinating. It's quite a long time since I saw your little niece.

ELIZABETH *(drily)* It must be. My " little " niece is twenty-one, and no longer grubby. She and Prudence are out somewhere, but they'll be back presently. How are you, Bertha? Sit down.

BERTHA *(putting the shopping list in her bag)* No, can't sit down. Mustn't stop. I only came just to see your mother for a moment, and wish her all the best and all that. Isn't she up yet?

ELIZABETH Oh, yes, she's up, but she's not down. She's pottering about her room—she potters for hours. *(She picks up the books from the chair R. and takes them to the bookcase, then crosses to table U.L. as she talks.)* Go up and see her.

BERTHA All right, I'll run up for a minute. You stay and talk to Elizabeth, Timothy. Shan't be long. *(She goes out R. TIMOTHY wanders round the room, helps himself to a cigarette from a box on the top of the bookcase U.R. and sits on the arm of the armchair C. ELIZABETH, with her back to him, goes on dusting.)*

ELIZABETH Sorry, Timothy, but I must get finished in here before Mother comes down. Sit down somewhere. Have a cigarette.

TIMOTHY *(pausing as he lights the cigarette)* Er . . . thanks. *(He finishes lighting the cigarette, and gazes reflectively at ELIZABETH's back.)* Poor old Liz!

ELIZABETH *(turning round)* Now, what exactly do you mean by that?

TIMOTHY Just that—poor old Liz. Whenever I see you, you're running round like a scalded cat on someone else's behalf. It must be one hell of a life, tied hand and foot to a couple of museum pieces.

ELIZABETH *(coming down C. towards him)* Are you referring to my parents? You're quite right, of course, but it's not for you to say so. And I'm sick of people being sorry for me. Even Florrie's been at it this morning.

TIMOTHY Good old Flo. What were her views?

ELIZABETH Oh, she only said . . . Go and sit somewhere else a minute, I want to straighten that chair. *(TIMOTHY moves to the armchair R., and ELIZABETH plumps up cushions and straightens covers)* Florrie was kind enough to say I ought to get married— no, to *have got* married. She evidently thought it was too late to do anything about it now.

TIMOTHY *(after a slight pause)* Do you agree with her—about its being too late, I mean? *(ELIZABETH stops dead, looks at him,*

*opens her mouth to say something, and then turns away and hammers
cushions furiously)* What's the matter?

ELIZABETH Nothing's the matter. Mind your own business, that's
all.

TIMOTHY Well, actually, it *is* my business. At least, I rather hope
it is. This is a funny time to get on the subject, but you started
it, and I have to seize my opportunities. Elizabeth . . .

ELIZABETH Do get out of the way, Timothy, I want to do round
there now. *(TIMOTHY goes to sofa L. and sits, and ELIZABETH
repeats the performance with cushions in the chair R.)*

TIMOTHY Lizzie, do listen. I tried to lead up to this last time I
was down, but you never gave me an opening. I . . .

ELIZABETH I do wish men could sit in a chair without pulling the
covers all over the place. *(She viciously tucks in the loose cover.)*

TIMOTHY Damn and blast, Elizabeth, will you listen to me for a
minute? I'm trying to ask you to marry me.

ELIZABETH And Father *will* spill tobacco ash all over them, which
doesn't help. They look like . . . *(She pauses, with a cushion in
her hand) . . . What* did you say?

TIMOTHY Nothing much. I said I was asking you to marry me,
that's all.

ELIZABETH *(putting the cushion back in the chair)* Oh, I see . . .
Don't be silly, Timothy, I haven't time to talk nonsense.

TIMOTHY Lizzie, my sweet, it isn't nonsense. I mean it. I've
meant it for ages. *(He gets up, goes over to ELIZABETH, and
seizes her by the arms from behind)* Now, leave the chores and
concentrate. Did you hear what I said?

ELIZABETH Yes, I heard. *(She turns and faces him)* Do you mean
you're seriously asking me to marry *you?*

TIMOTHY Well, you needn't make it sound as if I had a squint or
something. I know I'm not much to look at, but . . .

ELIZABETH It isn't that.

TIMOTHY Thanks very much. Any way, will you?

ELIZABETH *(breaking away from him)* No, of course not.

TIMOTHY Oh . . . Why not?

ELIZABETH Oh, don't be *stupid*, Timothy.

TIMOTHY Why *not?*

ELIZABETH Well, you're such an infant, for one thing—years
younger than I am.

TIMOTHY Thirty-four is hardly an infant. And you're what—forty,
perhaps.

ELIZABETH *(coldly)* Thirty-eight.

TIMOTHY Sorry. But there you are, you see. What's the
difference?

ELIZABETH Four years, if my arithmetic is correct. And four years
on the wrong side.

TIMOTHY Oh, rot. Four years is nothing. My Mamma was well
over thirty when she married, and five years older than my late

7

lamented Papa. It worked all right.

ELIZABETH I dare say it did. She probably hadn't known him in his cradle. Why, I remember when you stayed with us when you were about two, Nanny let me help to *bath* you.

TIMOTHY *(outraged)* Really, Elizabeth, these reminiscences are neither relevant nor—nor seemly.

ELIZABETH *(sitting on arm of chair R.)* She let me rinse the soap off. *(FLORRIE enters R.)* I can remember it now, squeezing water down your back with the sponge. I loved it. So did you, now I come to think of it.

FLORRIE *(coming down C.)* Excuse me, Miss Allen.

TIMOTHY Damn and blast! *(He goes and sits on sofa L.)*

FLORRIE Pardon?

ELIZABETH That's all right, Florrie—I mean, Mr. Todd was talking to me.

FLORRIE Yes, of course, Miss Allen . . . It's the Vicar, Miss Allen.

ELIZABETH What is?

FLORRIE He's hanging on to the telephone. Didn't you hear it ring? Well, I thought you couldn't of, so I just wiped my hands and ran down from the bathroom, and he says not to bother you if you're busy, but was his auntie here by any chance, so . . .

ELIZABETH Does he want to speak to Mrs. Todd?

FLORRIE Oh, gracious, no, I shouldn't think so. But he said if she was still here, and I said I thought she was, could you let her have the report about the hole the Guides made in the Parish Room floor, because he wants to go through it.

ELIZABETH Tell him he's had it.

FLORRIE *(hesitating)* Oh . . . Well, what shall I say, Miss Allen? I mean, I can't just say " You've had it," like that—not to the Vicar, can I?

ELIZABETH Don't be silly, Florrie—I mean I gave it to him days ago . . . All right, I'd better speak to him myself.

(ELIZABETH goes out R.)

FLORRIE *(lingering coyly)* Good morning, Mr. Todd. It's ever so nice to see you again, if you don't mind me saying so.

TIMOTHY Thank you, Florrie. Er . . . nice to see you again, too.

FLORRIE *(sitting on arm of chair C.)* I expect Miss Allen is glad to see you. Someone different, as you might say. She doesn't have much of a life, and anyone makes a change, don't they?

TIMOTHY *(meekly)* Oh, yes, anyone.

FLORRIE It's a shame, really. I like Miss Allen, don't you? I was only saying this morning—I like working for you, I said. Not like that old so-and-so at the . . . *(an embarrassed titter, as she realises what she has nearly said)* . . . . Oh, well, it takes all sorts to make a world, but when you think of some people it seems a pity.

TIMOTHY What does?

FLORRIE Well, that Miss Allen should be just an old maid, when she's quite nice, and lots of people who aren't so nice aren't, if you see what I mean.

TIMOTHY I think so. Well, being an old maid isn't necessarily a chronic affliction. It can be remedied.

FLORRIE Pardon? . . . Oh, I see what you mean. You do talk lovely sometimes. I suppose it's being a schoolteacher and that . . . . We-ell, as to that, where there's life there's hope, as they say. But in Miss Allen's case . . . Oh, my goodness, I've just thought! *(She springs to her feet.)*

TIMOTHY And *that's* a shock to the system, obviously.

FLORRIE You're telling me! I believe I left the tap running in the bathroom when I answered the phone! *(She rushes out R., colliding with* ELIZABETH, *who is coming in R.)* Sorry, Miss Allen, but it'll be through the ceiling of the downstairs lav.

ELIZABETH *(closing the door)* What'll be through the ceiling of the downstairs lav?

TIMOTHY The bathwater, I think. Have you settled Charles' difficulties?

ELIZABETH Oh, yes, he found it on his desk, under the " Church Times." He spent several minutes apologising for wasting my time. That's why I've been so long.

TIMOTHY For an otherwise intelligent man, my dear cousin Charles is one of the vaguest people I know. I always expect him to arrive in the pulpit and find he's forgotten his sermon. Actually, I don't think it's ever happened . . . *(He rises)* Now, let's get back to what we were talking about.

ELIZABETH What were we talking about?

TIMOTHY Elizabeth, you really are one of the most *maddening* women.

ELIZABETH Well, I'm sorry, Timothy, but there really is no more to say. I've told you " No." I must go and do the laundry. *(She goes to pick up the vacuum cleaner, but* TIMOTHY *intercepts her and brings her down C.)*

TIMOTHY Damn the laundry . . . Listen, darling, I *am* serious. Apart from—well—other considerations, I'm longing to take you away from all this.

ELIZABETH All what?

TIMOTHY Running round doing things for everybody, and never being able to call your soul your own. All these blasted domestic chores . . .

ELIZABETH Married women have domestic chores. Haven't you noticed?

TIMOTHY Yes, I know, but that's different. And it isn't only the domestic chores. Look at all you've got involved in besides, a slave to the whole village as well as your parents. Parish Magazines and—and Jumble Sales for Charles, Women's Institutes and Mothers' *Onions* . . .

ELIZABETH I do not belong to the *Mothers'* Union.

9

TIMOTHY   Well, the Girls' Friendly Society, if you think that's more suitable.   But above all, everything you do at home as well. Tied to your father and mother, never able to get away from everything.   It's hell.
(There is a short pause, as ELIZABETH *sits on chair R.)*

ELIZABETH *(slowly and rather bitterly)*   It's very kind of you to be sorry for me.   Is that why you're asking me to marry you?

TIMOTHY   Of course it isn't.   It isn't that at all, really.   It's just that . . . well, I do love you, you know, Lizzie.

ELIZABETH   Oh, Timothy, I'm sorry.   I didn't mean to be . . . But any way, it's impossible.

TIMOTHY   Why?   Because you can't leave the Parish Magazines and the Jumble Sales?

ELIZABETH   No, of course not.   I do those things for fun, but . . .

TIMOTHY   For *what?*

ELIZABETH   Well, for a change, then, to get me out of the house, so that I don't go mad.   But I *am* tied to Father and Mother, and I can't leave them completely alone.   There's no one else to look after them.

TIMOTHY   Can't the others take a hand?

ELIZABETH   What others?

TIMOTHY *(sitting C.)*   My sweet, to my knowledge, you have a brother and two sisters.   Your parents are just as much their responsibility as yours.

ELIZABETH   Yes, but they're all married, and with homes of their own.   Any way, they're mostly scattered all over the globe. Joanna is in America, and James settled in South Africa.   They can't even be here for the golden wedding.

TIMOTHY   And what about Prudence?

ELIZABETH   Prudence?

TIMOTHY   Now she's divorced her husband, why can't she come home and do her stuff?

ELIZABETH   Can you *see* Prudence?

TIMOTHY   I don't see why not.   She's had her fun.

ELIZABETH   Well, she wouldn't.   Not Prudence.   It's no *use*, Timothy.   Any way, I can't marry you, *really* I can't.   I'm sorry, but . . .

TIMOTHY   Is that final?

ELIZABETH *(rising)*   Absolutely . . . I'm *sorry*, Timothy.

TIMOTHY   So am I.   *(He rises and walks to the french window and looks out.   There is a pause.)*

ELIZABETH   I . . . expect your mother will be back presently.   Sit down again.

TIMOTHY   No, thanks.   *(He starts to move through the french window.)*

ELIZABETH   Where are you going?

TIMOTHY   Into the garden.   *(He goes out slowly L. of the window, and* ELIZABETH *takes a step towards the window.)*

ELIZABETH Timothy, I . . .
(*But* TIMOTHY *has gone, and* ELIZABETH *stands quite still, looking after him. Voices are heard off R., and* BERTHA *comes in R., followed by* MAUD *and* TOM. MAUD, *at 74, has decided to grow old gracefully, and dresses the part, with wisps of chiffon round the neck, rather long skirts, and a plaintive manner.* TOM, *although nearly ten years older, is still full of zest, if a trifle vague. He goes up to the table U.L. and examines the parcels.*)

MAUD Oh, there you are, Elizabeth. (*She looks round the room*) Oh dear, I thought you'd have finished in here by this time, but it doesn't matter. We can . . . What's the matter?

ELIZABETH Matter? Oh, nothing. I was just thinking. (*She turns and starts to collect the vacuum cleaner, etc.*)

MAUD Well, you know best, my dear, but I shouldn't have thought the middle of the morning was *quite* the time . . . Sit down, Bertha. (*MAUD sits in chair R.*)

BERTHA (*crossing L. and picking up her basket*) No, mustn't stop. I've been here far longer than I meant to as it is. Where's Timothy?

ELIZABETH (*moving towards door R., carrying the vacuum cleaner*) Timothy? Oh, he—went into the garden.

BERTHA Oh, how tiresome. Whatever for?

ELIZABETH To eat worms, I think. (*She goes out R.*)

BERTHA What an extraordinary thing!

TOM What? Eating worms? Oh, I don't know. I knew a Frenchman once who . . .

BERTHA Don't be an ass, Tom. I meant Elizabeth and Timothy. It sounds as if they'd been scrapping. They're generally the best of friends.

MAUD Elizabeth's very touchy lately, I've noticed it myself. You can't expect consideration from young people, dear . . . Tom, leave those parcels alone.

TOM Aren't we going to open them?

MAUD Later, dear, when Bertha's gone.

BERTHA All right, I don't need a hint. I ought to have gone ages ago. Got to go and see Mrs. Blake about the Young Wives. That reminds me, I might speak to Blake about the hens at the same time. (*BERTHA starts to go out through the french window, just as* PRUDENCE *and* SALLY *enter, followed by* TIMOTHY. BERTHA *backs into the room again with a deep sigh.* PRUDENCE *is a very well-preserved 43, rather too perfectly turned out for the country.* SALLY, *an attractive 21, is more suitably dressed.*)

PRUDENCE (*languidly*) Bertha, my dear, too lovely to see you. (*She offers a cheek, which* BERTHA *ignores*) The garden's looking divine. We found Timothy there. (*She sits C.* TIMOTHY *wanders moodily round, and finally sits L. in sulky silence.* SALLY *joins* TOM *at the table U.L.*)

SALLY Sitting on the bird bath.

11

BERTHA Very bad for him. Hello, Sally, you're looking flourishing.
Too much muck on your face, as usual, like your mother. Sorry,
but I must go. See you tonight.

MAUD Oh, yes, and that reminds me. You're all staying to supper-
afterwards—you and Charles, and Timothy, of course, now he's
here.

BERTHA Oh, I don't know, Maud. Awful lot of extra work for
you.

MAUD No, of course not, dear. Elizabeth will see to it, so it won't
be any trouble to anybody. A little private party—just ourselves
and the bridesmaids. Emma will be here, too.

BERTHA Emma?

MAUD Oh, my dear, you remember little Emma Jelly. She was
one of the child bridesmaids with poor Marjorie.

BERTHA Oh, yes, the brat with adenoids.

MAUD I know, dear, but I had to ask her because of her mother
being a sort of cousin. It was rather awkward. They were *not*
a good-looking family. Her mother had the most dreadful poppy
sort of eyes, I remember. Any way, I expect she's had them out
long ago.

TOM Her eyes?

MAUD No, of course not. She died years ago. But I always kept
up with her and Emma from time to time, and when I thought of
having the bridesmaids to the golden wedding party, I wrote and
asked her to come and spend a day or two.

TOM I thought you said she was dead.

MAUD Oh, no, Tom, you're thinking of poor Marjorie. Tom
does get so mixed up . . . Poor Emma, she hasn't been very lucky.
She was left very badly off, and she's a companion to some tiresome
old woman or something. Very trying, I should think.

BERTHA Pretty grim . . . Look here, I must go. Come with us,
Sally. The walk'll do you good.

MAUD *(rising)* Why, it's such a lovely morning, I think I'll take a
little walk in the garden myself. We'll walk down the drive with
you. Come along, Tom.

TOM Come along where?

MAUD I told you, Tom. Bertha wants us to walk down the drive
with her. Don't keep her waiting . . . Now, I wonder if I ought
to have my coat. Elizabeth, go and . . . Oh dear, she's not here.
How tiresome.

SALLY I'll get it. Where is it?

MAUD No, dear, I wouldn't dream of troubling you. I shall be
all right, I expect. (ELIZABETH *enters R.)* Oh, there you are,
Elizabeth. Just run up to my bedroom and get my coat. The
brown one. Don't bring the blue, because I don't think you've
mended the lining for me yet. Bertha wants me to walk down
the drive with her.

BERTHA *(nearly bursting)* Maud, if you're coming, for goodness sake come along. You don't need a coat. It's as hot as hell in the sun.

MAUD Is it, dear? Oh, well, you know best about that. Perhaps I shall be all right, and Elizabeth does take so long to find things. Come along, Tom, you're keeping Bertha waiting. *(BERTHA marches out through the french window, followed by MAUD and TOM. SALLY looks uncertainly at TIMOTHY, who gets up slowly. He catches her eye, suddenly appears to pull himself together, and smiles at her.)*

TIMOTHY Coming?

(TIMOTHY and SALLY go out through the french window. PRUDENCE takes a compact from her bag and repairs her face. ELIZABETH watches the family from the window, then turns to PRUDENCE and hesitates.)

PRUDENCE Don't let me keep you if you've things to do. I can amuse myself.

ELIZABETH *(sweetly)* You generally can, dear, I know that. And I *have* got things to do, but if they're going to stay out for a bit it's an opportunity to catch you alone. I want to talk to you.

PRUDENCE What about?

ELIZABETH Wait a minute. *(She rushes out R. PRUDENCE rises and takes a cigarette and a magazine from the top of the bookcase U.R. She lights the cigarette, and sits C. again, opening the magazine. ELIZABETH reappears R. staggering under a laundry basket oozing crumpled sheets, towels, and other articles. She has a laundry book in her mouth, and a pencil behind the ear.)*

PRUDENCE What on earth . . . ?

ELIZABETH *(looking round for somewhere to put the laundry, and speaking indistinctly with the laundry book still in her mouth)* I thought I could do this while I was talking to you. *(She dumps the basket on the floor L.C., takes the clothes out and scatters them round it, removes the book from her mouth, and squats on the floor.)*

PRUDENCE Really, Elizabeth, *must* you bring that sordid collection in here? And a pencil behind the ear is the *end*.

ELIZABETH *(removing the pencil)* It was the only place for it at that moment. And I'm sorry if bath-towels and Father's pyjamas offend your eyes, but I must get it done before the man comes at twelve. I thought I could do it while I was talking to you, and save time.

PRUDENCE What do you want to talk about?

ELIZABETH Me. And you.

PRUDENCE What have I done?

ELIZABETH You haven't—yet. It's what I want you to do. Wait a minute—three sheets. *(She writes in the book, and stuffs the sheets into the basket)* Listen, Pru, it's really about me and the parents. I'm just about at the end of my tether.

PRUDENCE *(yawning)* Sounds like a goat.

13

ELIZABETH *(crossly)* Very funny. Ha, ha. But as a matter of fact, I've come to the conclusion that I *am* a goat to have put up with it all these years.

PRUDENCE Put up with what?

ELIZABETH Being tied up. Ever since Mother was ill, twelve years ago, and I came home to nurse her, I've just *stayed* at home till they took it for granted. And lately I've gradually realised that they've grown old, and can't be left, and that it's a life sentence for me. I might as well be a nun or something . . . Three bath-towels. *(She stuffs two towels in the basket)* Damn, where's the other?

PRUDENCE You're kneeling on it.

ELIZABETH Oh, yes. Thanks. *(She puts it in and writes in the book)* So that's what I really wanted to talk to you about.

PRUDENCE My dear, I'm glad you got it off your chest, if you feel that way about it; but I don't see what one can do about it. I quite agree that the parents can't be left on their own at their age. But you're the obvious person to look after them, after all.

ELIZABETH Am I?

PRUDENCE Of course you are. You're their daughter.

ELIZABETH So are you.

PRUDENCE Me?

ELIZABETH Yes, you. You're as much their daughter as I am. I admit I hadn't thought of that solution myself, but actually Timothy put the idea into my head. He said . . .

PRUDENCE Timothy? Have you been discussing this with Timothy?

ELIZABETH *(sorting laundry)* Well . . . it sort of came up in the course of conversation. He pointed out that now Roderick has divorced you . . .

PRUDENCE Well, I'm damned! Roderick did nothing of the sort. I divorced *him*.

ELIZABETH *(airily)* Oh, well, that's a mere quibble. He probably let you—Roderick was always the perfect little gentleman. Actually, I always rather liked Roderick. Pity to lose him out of the family, really . . . Six table napkins. *(She counts and writes.)*

PRUDENCE My dear, Roderick was *always* a mistake. I married far too young, of course—straight out of the schoolroom, one might say.

ELIZABETH One might. But if you were still in the schoolroom at twenty-one, you were more backward even than I thought . . . One pair of pyjamas and one afternoon tea-cloth. What a funny mixture laundry is, when you come to think of it.

PRUDENCE Any way, I stuck to Roderick for over twenty years, and I think that says a good deal for me.

ELIZABETH Mmmm . . . It says something for Roderick, too, when you come to think of it.

PRUDENCE My God, if you're as fond of Roderick as all that, you'd better marry him yourself. You're very welcome.

ELIZABETH Thanks ... One perfectly filthy roller towel. I wonder what Florrie does with them . . . I don't think I will, though. Wouldn't it be a Deceased Wife's Sister or something? Though I believe that doesn't matter nowadays.

PRUDENCE You needn't add to your other insults by calling me " deceased." Any way, I don't know how we got on to this subject, but I imagine you didn't bring that disgusting collection in here merely to talk about my private affairs.

ELIZABETH *(becoming serious)* No . . . No, I didn't. Sorry, Pru, I don't know why we always fight as soon as we get together for five minutes. We rub each other up the wrong way every time.

PRUDENCE And yet, if I understood what you were getting at just now, you're suggesting that I should come and live here and help with the parents. We could then fight *all* the time. It *would* be fun.

ELIZABETH Oh, no, it wouldn't . . . I mean, I shouldn't be here. I'm suggesting that you should take my place, so that I could get away.

PRUDENCE Get away? Where to?

ELIZABETH *(after a pause)* This is in strict confidence. Is that understood?

PRUDENCE You can trust me. I wasn't called Prudence for nothing.

ELIZABETH How true. Well, then, I . . . want to get married.

PRUDENCE To get *what?*

ELIZABETH You heard—to get married. Don't look so surprised. Quite a lot of people do it.

PRUDENCE I know, but I should have thought by this time . . .

ELIZABETH All right, all right. I know all about that. But in spite of—er—my advanced years and apparently confirmed spinster hood, I have received what I believe used to be called an Offer. An offer I . . . should very much like to accept. Not from Roderick, incidentally.

PRUDENCE *(rising and going to an ashtray to stub out her cigarette)* So I supposed. Are you going to tell me who it is?

ELIZABETH That I am *not* going to tell you. At the moment I've refused it any way.

PRUDENCE Because of Father and Mother?

ELIZABETH *(quietly)* Yes, because of Father and Mother.

PRUDENCE *(coming down C. again)* I see . . . Well, I must say I never thought of such a thing, but it's possible, I suppose. And you've know each other all your life, more or less.

ELIZABETH *(rising)* You mean—you've guessed who it is?

PRUDENCE You rather gave it away yourself, didn't you? Something you let out earlier in this interesting conversation.

ELIZABETH Something *I* let out? I haven't even mentioned . . . Look here, Pru, I . . . *(She stops as voices are heard outside the french window)* Oh, damn, damn, damn!

15

PRUDENCE *(sitting C. and taking up the magazine again)* Mamma won't approve of sheets and pyjamas in the drawing room.

ELIZABETH I don't care what she approves of; but we shan't be able to talk any more, so I may as well go. *(She shuts the lid of the basket, which she has now finished packing, and picks it up in her arms, leaving the laundry book on the floor)* I'll talk to you again later if I get a chance.

PRUDENCE My dear, if you're thinking of my coming here and taking your place at home, it really can't be done. I don't think you realise what you're asking. Sorry, but there it is. You'll have to think of some other solution.

ELIZABETH *(going towards the door R.)* I've thought of them all, and there aren't any. *(MAUD and TOM enter through the french window)* And if you mention this to *anyone*, I'll kill you.

TOM *(with mild interest)* What are you going to kill her for? *(ELIZABETH goes out R. TOM returns to the parcels U.L.)*

MAUD *(sitting R.)* Don't be silly, Tom, Elizabeth really hasn't time for that sort of thing in the middle of the morning. There's too much to do. What's that on the floor?

PRUDENCE The laundry book, I should think.

MAUD How extraordinary. How on earth did it get there? Pick it up, dear, it looks so untidy, and Emma will be here soon. *(PRUDENCE picks up the book and stuffs it down the side of her chair)* I hope Elizabeth remembered to order the taxi to meet her. She's so forgetful, and I really can't think of everything. Tom, leave those parcels alone.

TOM Aren't we going to open the damn things?

MAUD Later, dear, I thought it would be nice to open them when we're all together before lunch. It'll be something to amuse Emma.

TOM Who's Emma? *(He leaves the parcels reluctantly and moves down L. to below sofa, taking a pipe and tobacco pouch from his pocket.)*

MAUD I told you, Tom. She's coming to stay.

TOM Oh, I see . . . *(He blows through his pipe with loud and succulent noises, and begins to fill and light it)* Do I know her?

MAUD Of course you do; she was one of the bridesmaids. Though I dare say she's altered a good deal. She was about ten then, I think. *(FLORRIE enters R. and comes L. of MAUD)* I don't know whether I shall recognise her . . . What is it, Florrie?

FLORRIE She's come.

MAUD Who?

FLORRIE Miss Whatsername. Didn't you hear the taxi? It's a wonder you didn't, the noise Fred Golding makes with that old tin can of his. Why, I . . .

MAUD Do you mean Miss Jelly's arrived?

FLORRIE That's the one.

MAUD Well, really, Florrie, if you answer the door, do please show

16

people in properly, and announce their names. And don't leave them waiting in the hall. Ask Miss Jelly to come in.

FLORRIE *(turning towards the door R.)* O.K., Mrs. Allen.

MAUD And Florrie—(FLORRIE *comes back)*—I don't want to be *too* fussy, but you know I detest that expression. And I've told you before—don't keep calling me " Mrs. Allen." It is *not* the proper way to address me.

FLORRIE Oh, I know what you mean, Mrs. Allen. It's just like my Mum. Only the other day, she said the same to our lodger. " I wish you wouldn't call me ' Mrs. Parkinson ' every time," she says. " The name's Gertie," she says . . .

MAUD *(almost speechless)* That will do, Florrie. Ask Miss Jelly to come in at *once.*

FLORRIE O.K., Mrs. Allen. *(She goes to the door R., puts her head out, and calls)* Mrs. Allen says you're to come in at *once,* Miss Jelly.

(FLORRIE stands aside, but remains in the room as EMMA JELLY enters R. She is about 60, pleasant-looking and plainly dressed, with nothing remarkable about her appearance, not even traces of the youthful adenoids. As she comes in, she catches sight of SALLY and TIMOTHY, who are just entering by the french window. EMMA gives a start, and, taking no notice of anyone else, rushes towards TIMOTHY.)

EMMA *Wilfred!*

TOM Wilfred? Where?

TIMOTHY Are you—talking to me?

TOM Who *is* Wilfred? *(To TIMOTHY)* Your name's not Wilfred, is it?

EMMA *(recovering herself)* No . . . No, of course not, you couldn't be. I really do beg your pardon; you just gave me rather a shock for the moment. You're so very, very like him.

TOM *(sitting L. on the sofa)* Like who? That lad's the spit and image of his father—always was. No doubt about who *his* father was, I always said so. Luckily for old Bertha. *(He gives a coarse laugh, which is ill-received by MAUD.)*

MAUD That will do, Florrie. *(FLORRIE goes out R. reluctantly.)*

EMMA Yes, of course . . . That might explain . . . Do forgive me, but is your name Todd, by any chance?

TIMOTHY *(still bewildered)* Yes, it is, as a matter of fact, but . . .

EMMA And your father's name is Wilfred?

TIMOTHY Well, he—er—he couldn't help it, you know, but—yes, I'm afraid it was.

EMMA *(almost in a whisper)* Was . . . ?

TIMOTHY Was? Oh, I see what you mean. Oh, yes, he . . .
(ELIZABETH bursts in R.)

ELIZABETH *(coming down C.)* Did I drop the laundry book in here? *(She looks frantically about the floor)* Oh, heavens, where is the damn thing? The man's here, and I can't find it anywhere.

PRUDENCE *(taking the book from her chair)* Is this what you're looking for?

ELIZABETH What? Oh, there it is. Why couldn't you tell me? I've been looking for it all over the place, and you were sitting on it all the time.

PRUDENCE You left it on the floor.

ELIZABETH There! I knew I had it safely, and you go and hide it. *(She starts to go out R. and turns back)* Oh, lend me some money, someone. I haven't enough change, and I want to pay the laundry. *(She crosses L. to* TOM*)* Father, have you got one and three ha'pence?

TOM What do you want one and three ha'pence for?

ELIZABETH I *told* you. To pay the laundry.

TOM Is that all it is? I thought laundries had gone up. Your mother said . . .

ELIZABETH I want one and three ha'pence *more*.

TOM More than what?

ELIZABETH More than I've got. Oh, hurry up, Father, the man's waiting.

TOM *(fumbling in his pocket, and counting out change)* That reminds me, you already owe me three bob.

ELIZABETH No, I don't, it was two and tenpence. I'll pay you back later. Thanks. *(She takes the money and rushes out R. colliding with* FLORRIE, *who is entering R.* TOM *takes his pipe out of his mouth and drops off to sleep.)*

FLORRIE *(with exaggerated ceremony)* The—Reveren*t*—Fairfax! *(This formal announcement is rather marred by the fact that* FLORRIE *immediately collides with* CHARLES FAIRFAX *in the doorway R. She disentangles herself and goes out, and* CHARLES *enters. He is about 45, and, except for his collar, there is nothing aggressively clerical about his appearance. He is slightly untidy, with a button missing from his jacket.)*
*(*EMMA *has retreated to the back of the room with* TIMOTHY *and* SALLY, *and* MAUD, *her attention distracted by* CHARLES' *entrance, seems to have forgotten all about her.* EMMA *looks helplessly at* SALLY *and* TIMOTHY, *and hovers uncertainly.)*

MAUD Oh, Charles how nice. Come in.

CHARLES *(looking round and glancing hesitatingly at* EMMA*)* Oh, I say, I'm frightfully sorry. I didn't know you had . . . Hello, Prudence, how are you? And Sally. *(He looks again at* EMMA *and then at* MAUD, *expecting an introduction. As this is not forthcoming, he vaguely murmurs "How do you do?" in* EMMA'S *direction.)*

MAUD We're always pleased to see you, Charles. Sit down.

CHARLES *(unhappily)* No . . No, really, I can easily come another time. It isn't urgent.

MAUD Nonsense. I'm not in the least busy. What is it?

CHARLES *(coming L. of* MAUD*)* We-ell . . . Well, I merely wanted to consult you about something—nothing confidential, really, at least I don't see why it should be, because I don't think there is such a person, but I wanted to make sure.

MAUD I'm afraid I don't quite understand.

CHARLES No . . . No, I was afraid you wouldn't. It's just that I've had a—a rather embarrassing letter from a strange woman.

SALLY Tut, tut!

MAUD Be quiet, dear. You mustn't interrupt when grown-up people are talking. Go and play in the garden while we talk. *(SALLY, with a grin at TIMOTHY, goes out through the french window, and TIMOTHY follows. EMMA looks after them unhappily, and is left unnoticed U.S.)* What sort of letter, Charles?

CHARLES Well, it's . . . *(He fumbles in his pocket, takes out a letter, and hands it to MAUD)* Perhaps you would read it, and see if you can help me.
(MAUD takes the letter, puts on her glasses, and starts to read. She looks increasingly bewildered.)

MAUD But I still don't understand. *(She begins to read aloud in a puzzled voice)* " Dear Reverend Fairfax, About the twins, me and their father thinks they should be . . .

CHARLES Oh . . . Oh dear, *no*. I'm so sorry, that must be Mrs. Farrow's letter about the christening. *(He takes it from MAUD, feels in another pocket, and takes out another letter and looks at it)* Yes, this is the one. You see it's addressed just to " The Incumbent, Ashfield." Actually, it was a day or two before they delivered it to me. Miss Carter at the Post Office didn't quite know what " Incumbent " meant.

MAUD *(reading aloud)* " Dear Sir, Forgive me for troubling you, but I am wondering if you can tell me the correct name of a Mrs. Allison or possibly Collins, who I understand resides in your parish . . ." Well, which does she mean? Nobody can be called Allison *or* Collins.

CHARLES That's what she's trying to find out. Read on.

MAUD *(reading)* " I was recently obliged to dismiss without notice my mother's companion-housekeeper, for reasons with which I will not trouble you with . . ." With which I will not trouble you with . . . ?
(EMMA, in the background, gives a start, and during the reading of the rest of the letter shows increasing agitation.)

CHARLES Yes, it's a bit muddled, but I think I see what she means. Go on.

MAUD " My mother has revealed that this person, from something she let out in the course of conversation, was proposing to betake herself "—what a funny expression—" betake herself to the village of Ashfield, presumably to a similar post. She is ninety-four . . . ." Oh, surely not. No one would employ a woman of that age.

CHARLES I think she means her mother is ninety-four.

MAUD Oh . . . Why doesn't she say so then? . . . " ninety-four, and very active for her age, but her memory is not what it was, and she does not seem quite certain of the name of this person's new employer, but thinks it was either Collins or Allison. The name of the village she is quite certain about, as Ashfield was my dear mother's own maiden name, and she remembers that perfectly . . . " Yes, I suppose she might . . . " I shall be grateful if you can help me to trace this Mrs. Collins. Without wishing to be vindictive, I feel it is my duty as a Christian to expose the real character of this person, and to warn Mrs. Allison that she is being imposed on by an undesirable woman, who may even have written her own references. Can you kindly help me by telling me Mrs. Collins' name and address? Yours truly, Selina Crabtree."

(EMMA, *still unnoticed, lets out a long sigh, as if to say " I knew it !"*)

TOM *(opening his eyes)* Who's Selina Crabtree? Damn silly name. *(As no one takes any notice, he goes to sleep again.)*

MAUD " P.S.—My mother has since admitted that the name may possibly be Hanbury." . . . Charles, what is all this? Who *is* Selina Crabtree?

CHARLES Well, except that she seems to have a rather odd idea of her duty as a Christian, I really know nothing about her. She's obviously an old . . . er, that is to say, I think she's misguided in her intentions, but I thought I'd better answer the letter. I merely wanted to be able to tell her quite truthfully that I don't *know* a Mrs. Collins or a Mrs. Allison.

MAUD Or Hanbury.

CHARLES Or Hanbury. I . . .

TOM *(with his eyes shut)* Or Crabtree.

CHARLES I think I know everyone in the village, but you've been here so much longer than I have that I thought I'd just ask you before I wrote. Can you think of any one might be called Allison or Hanbury?

MAUD Or Collins. No . . . No, I can't at all.

CHARLES Well, that's all right, then. I can write back with a perfectly clear conscience and tell the woman she's mistaken. It's such a relief. I do hate busybodies. *(He takes the letter from* MAUD *and puts it back in his pocket.)*

MAUD Wasn't there a Mrs. Collins at the " Royal Oak " when we first came here? I never really knew her, because she died of drink soon afterwards. But that was fifty years ago, so I suppose it couldn't be the one.

CHARLES No, I'm sure it couldn't. Now I must go. Thank you so much. Goodbye. *(He glances diffidently at* EMMA.) Er . . . good morning. (CHARLES *starts to go out R.)*

MAUD We're looking forward to seeing you this evening, Charles.

CHARLES *(pausing)* This evening?

20

MAUD The party, you know. Our golden wedding party.

CHARLES Oh . . . Oh *dear!* *(He takes out a diary from his pocket and scratches through it.)*

PRUDENCE *(looking up for the first time)* I suppose you'd forgotten all about it. *(She gets up and looks over his shoulder.)*

CHARLES Oh, no No, indeed. *(He turns a page)* No, I've got it down.

PRUDENCE *(reading the diary over his shoulder)* So you have— " Mother Allen, Free Drinks, 6.15." *(CHARLES shuts the book hastily and makes for the door R., then turns back.)*

CHARLES Oh . . . and . . . I quite forgot. Congratulations to you both.

MAUD Thank you, Charles. Goodbye for the present. Prudence, see Charles out, dear. *(PRUDENCE gives her mother a Look, but goes out R. with CHARLES. TOM continues to sleep, and MAUD sits staring in front of her, still forgetting about EMMA, who hovers behind.)*

MAUD Collins—Allison—Hanbury . . . No, I really can't think . . . . *(EMMA gives a gentle cough, and MAUD turns round, sees her, and gets slowly and quite composedly to her feet.)* Why, of course, I knew there was something. You must be Emma. My dear, I shouldn't have known you. How do you do?

CURTAIN.

ACT II

The same evening.

(The room is lit by a single standard lamp. FLORRIE is going round collecting glasses on to a tray, and absentmindedly polishing off the dregs. She finds also a plate with two lonely-looking cocktail snacks, which she pops into her mouth, makes a face, and prepares to depart as voices are heard off R. FLORRIE swallows hastily, wipes her mouth, and backs D.L. as MAUD cautiously opens the door R. and peeps furtively into the room.)

MAUD Shoo! Sh-shoo!

BERTHA *(off R.)* What on earth . . . ? Is there a burglar or something?

MAUD *(with another look around)* No, I think it's all right. *(MAUD enters, followed by BERTHA, EMMA and PRUDENCE, and switches on the lights)* It's just that I thought I saw a mouse in here one evening, so I always take precautions after dark . . . *(FLORRIE knocks over a glass on the tray)* Good gracious, Florrie, how you startled me. Haven't you finished clearing up yet?

FLORRIE Just about, but a few bits and pieces got left behind, sort of, so I came back to collect them. I've done the rest, and would you believe it, I've only broken two. If you've finished supper, I'll wash that up before I go. May as well be hung for a sheep as a lamb.

MAUD The men are still in the dining-room, but I think Miss Allen and Miss Sally went into the kitchen to start washing up. I expect they'll help you. Oh . . . coffee . . . *(She looks round helplessly.)*

FLORRIE Did you want some coffee? O.K., I'll get it. *(She goes to the door R. and turns)* Ever such a nice party, wasn't it? I *did* enjoy it. *(FLORRIE goes out R.)*

MAUD *(sitting C.)* I cannot *think* why Elizabeth insists on keeping that girl.

EMMA She seems very good-natured. *(EMMA crosses to L. and sits on the sofa. BERTHA sits R., and PRUDENCE, looking bored and ignoring everyone, wanders to the french window and looks out.)*

MAUD Well, I suppose good nature's all right, up to a point. You don't know how lucky you are, Bertha, having Mrs. Wilkins.

BERTHA Nobody could accuse Mrs. Wilkins of being good-natured, any way.

MAUD Perhaps not, dear, but she's a nice, old-fashioned servant— bad-tempered in such a *respectful* way. It's quite refreshing these days. *I* think you're very fortunate to have her.

BERTHA *(hesitating, and then obviously making up her mind to speak)* Well, I shan't have her much longer—not at the Vicarage, any way.

MAUD My dear, why not? Surely she's not leaving after all these years.

BERTHA *She's* not. I am.

MAUD You're *what?*

BERTHA I'm leaving—or rather Charles is. It's a bit hush-hush
still, but most of the village knows, and he said I could tell you
in confidence. He's been offered a living in Nottinghamshire.

MAUD Dear me! Why?

BERTHA I can't think.

MAUD Nottinghamshire . . . How extraordinary. I thought that
was just coal mines and lace and things. Somehow I never
imagined any one *living* there . . . There was Robin Hood, of
course . . . My dear, will you like that?

BERTHA I'm not going.

MAUD Not going? But what about Charles?

BERTHA I suppose he'll have to have a housekeeper or something.
I've kept house for Charles for ten years—ever since he came
here—and it suited me very well after Wilfred died. But I'm not
living on top of a slag heap, and I've told Charles so quite firmly.

MAUD Oh dear, do you think you'll have to? It may not be all
coal mines.

BERTHA Perhaps not, but I want to stay in this part of the world.
Besides, there's another thing. I didn't tell you this before,
either, but Timothy's applied for rather a good job at that big
school at the top of Sutton Hill—St. Christopher's or whatever
it calls itself—and if he gets that it's non-resident, and I must make
a home for him somewhere here.

MAUD Oh . . . Oh dear, what a lot of changes. Where will you
live? I suppose you can't just stay on at the Vicarage—they'll
want that for someone else, won't they? What a pity; you're
so comfortable there.

BERTHA That's going to be the difficulty. I shall have to find a
small cottage somewhere here, and it won't be all that easy. If
I haven't found what I want by the time Charles goes, I was
wondering whether . . .

(FLORRIE enters R. with a tray of coffee and coffee cups.)

FLORRIE *(crossing to L.)* Here we are. Sorry I've been so long, but
better late than never, as they say. *(She puts the tray on the
table U.L.)* The Vicar's helping to wash up now, so Miss Allen
said I was to go when I'd brought this in. The others have had
theirs. *(She picks up the coffee pot)* Now, how does everyone
like it? Just as it comes?

MAUD *(rising and moving U.L.)* That will do, Florrie. I'll pour
out the coffee. You can go.

FLORRIE O.K., just as you like. *(MAUD takes the pot from her
and begins to pour out)* Well, may as well say bye-bye, then.
Nightie-night, all. *(FLORRIE goes out R.)*

MAUD *(starting to hand round the cups)* Oh, Emma, do you take
black or white?

EMMA Black, please. *(She rises, and goes towards MAUD.)*

MAUD Oh . . . Oh dear, I've given you white.

EMMA Oh, then, that will do beautifully. I like it just as well.

MAUD *(handing her the cup)* Are your sure? . . . Sugar?

EMMA Thank you . . . Yes, a little, please.

MAUD *(looking on the tray)* Oh dear—nobody else takes it, and Florrie's forgotten it. Prudence, dear, go and ask for some sugar. Emma takes *sugar* in her coffee. *(She manages to imply by this last remark that* EMMA *has thoroughly unpleasant habits.* PRUDENCE *makes a half-hearted move towards the door R. but returns to the window as* EMMA *protests.)*

EMMA Oh, no, *please.* I often have it without. I like it. *(She drinks her coffee at a gulp, rather as if it were a dose of medicine)* There! That was delicious. *(She puts the cup on the table, and resumes her seat L.)*

MAUD *(drinking hers)* It's perfectly horrible. It's nearly cold. I'm so sorry, Bertha, I can't think why Elizabeth can't make decent coffee. *(She puts down her cup)* Oh, Bertha, you must come up and see my lovely presents. They're in my room. Come along now, while we're alone. *(*BERTHA *rises, and she and* MAUD *go towards the door R.* EMMA *also rises and makes as if to go with them, then hesitates.* MAUD *turns and sees her)* Oh, Emma, would you like to come too?

EMMA Oh . . thank you . . . No, please don't bother. I'll stay here and *(with a doubtful look at* PRUDENCE, *who is still taking no notice of anyone)* talk to Prudence.

MAUD All right. Well, make yourself comfortable. Do you smoke?

EMMA I . . Yes, I do sometimes.

MAUD *(disapprovingly)* Oh. Well, have a cigarette. Prudence give Emma a cigarette. I think there are some in that box. I *never* smoke myself, but do have one. *(*TOM *and* TIMOTHY *enter R.)* Oh, Tom, we're just going to look at my presents.

TOM *Our* presents.

MAUD It's the same thing, dear. Come along, Bertha.

*(*MAUD *and* BERTHA *go out R.* PRUDENCE *offers the cigarettes to* EMMA, *who smiles and shakes her head.* PRUDENCE *offers one to* TIMOTHY *and takes one herself.* TIMOTHY *lights them both* TOM *sits L. and closes his eyes,* EMMA *hesitates and then sits diffidently C., and* PRUDENCE *walks back to the french window.)*

PRUDENCE   It's a heavenly evening. I simply can't stay indoors. Timothy, come for a breather in the garden.

TIMOTHY Oh . . . Well, don't you think we ought to stay here? Where is everyone?

PRUDENCE Washing up, I think. Come on—there's a lovely moon.

TIMOTHY *(guardedly)* Yes, I know. What about helping with the washing up?

PRUDENCE My dear, don't be morbid. There's a scrum in the

kitchen already. Come on. Any way, I want to talk to you.

TIMOTHY Oh Lord! *(He follows reluctantly, and he and* PRUDENCE *go out through the french window. As they do so,* CHARLES *enters R. He is quite tidily dressed for once, in a dark suit with all the buttons intact, but there is a frilly apron round his middle.)*

CHARLES Oh, hello. All alone? *(He notices* TOM *who is peacefully sleeping)* Well, more or less, any way. They said I was in the way while they finished up, so they sent me in here. I've been helping to dry.

EMMA *(with a smile at the apron)* So I see.

CHARLES What? . . . Oh dear, that's Elizabeth's fault. She made me put it on to protect what she kindly calls my one decent suit. *(He removes the apron, throws it in a corner, and sits R.)* Well, jolly good party, wasn't it? I hope you enjoyed it.

EMMA Very much, thank you. I think I had too much to drink.

CHARLES I beg your pardon?

EMMA I'm not really used to cocktails. And I had two.

CHARLES I had four—I think. They were particularly innocuous.

EMMA Yes, that's what I thought at the time. Isn't there something they call " delayed action "—or am I thinking of bombs? . . . Mr. Fairfax, while we're . . *(She glances at the sleeping* TOM *and then leans R. towards* CHARLES*)* . . alone, I would like to talk to you. I—I want to make a confession.

CHARLES *(looking alarmed, and half rising)* Oh dear . . . I mean, I shall be only too happy to . . er . . .

EMMA Oh, not officially, of course. I wouldn't dream of asking you to talk business at a party. It's just something I thought I'd like to explain.

CHARLES *(sitting back, and taking a pipe from his pocket)* Yes?

EMMA It's that letter you brought this morning—the one from Mrs. Crabtree. I thought I ought to tell you that it was me—I mean, it was I.

CHARLES *(beginning to fill his pipe)* *You* wrote it?

EMMA Oh dear me, no. I mean I'm the companion-housekeeper she dismissed. You see, for nearly twenty years now I've been housekeeper to Mrs. Crabtree's mother, Mrs. Robinson. I'm very, very fond of her—Mrs. Robinson, I mean, not Mrs. Crabtree.

CHARLES I imagined that was what you meant. Go on.

EMMA Mrs. Robinson was fond of me, too, though perhaps I shouldn't say so. She depended on me. Mrs. Crabtree—her daughter, you know—lived in Scotland until recently, and we hardly ever saw her. Then, a few months ago, she came south to live.

CHARLES And you and Mrs. Crabtree didn't get on?

EMMA *(earnestly)* It really wasn't my fault, you know. Mrs. Crabtree is a very odd sort of woman.

CHARLES Her letter rather gave me that impression.

EMMA Mrs. Robinson is quite well off, you see—not so well off as

25

she used to be, of course, because nobody is—and Mrs. Crabtree seemed to think that she might leave me her money.

CHARLES She thought you were—er—scki ng up to Mrs. Robinson.

EMMA How funny—that's one of the expressions *she* used. She used another one, too. I can't remember exactly what it was, but it sounded extremely unladylike. I can't think how a woman of her age *knows* all those words. I don't.

CHARLES I'm sure you don't. *(He feels in his pocket for matches, finds none, and rises to get the box of matches from the top of the bookcase U.R. Having lighted the pipe, he puts the matches absentmindedly in his own pocket, and comes D.R. beside* EMMA'S *chair as she goes on talking.)*

EMMA Mrs. Crabtree was *extremely* rude, and in the end she dismissed me. Mrs. Robinson was very upset—very upset indeed. And that's what worries me.

CHARLES Tell me, how did Mrs. Crabtree know you were coming to Ashfield?

EMMA I expect she wormed it out of her mother. I had told Mrs. Robinson some time ago about Maud asking me here, and she was interested because of the name of the village. And I think she remembered part of what we'd talked about, and then got it muddled up in her mind. She did, you know. After all, she's ninety-four.

CHARLES *(sitting R.)* When did all this happen? Did you come straight here?

EMMA Oh, no, I couldn't. Maud hadn't asked me till today. I've been living in an hotel for nearly a week. I have a little money of my own, you see. Not much, but enough to tide me over.

CHARLES And—forgive my asking—what about when you leave here?

EMMA *(after a pause)* That's a—little difficult to say.

CHARLES If you want another job, I dare say I could help to . . .

EMMA But I don't, you see—not for the moment. Oh dear, it's rather difficult to explain, but—well—Mrs. Robinson did depend on me so. She was used to me, I suppose, and I know she won't be happy with anyone else. And I'm hoping—it sounds rather conceited, but I don't mean it like that—I'm hoping they'll find they can't do without me, and will ask me to come back for her sake. I feel I ought to—to stand by, as it were.

CHARLES But . . . I don't want to make difficulties, but if Mrs. Crabtree doesn't know where to find you, that won't be much use

EMMA I thought of that. I left an address with Mr. Carraway— he's Mrs. Robinson's solicitor.

CHARLES You seem to have thought of everything.

EMMA Oh, no, there's probably a lot I haven't thought of. And now I've told you, it sounds such a silly, trivial sort of story. But I thought I'd feel happier if I explained that I really hadn't done anything *wrong*.

CHARLES *(gently)* I never thought you had. The only thing that worries me is that for the moment you should be—well—homeless. How long are you staying here?

EMMA Well, I . . .

TOM *(opening his eyes)* Stay as long as you like. Love to have you. *(There is a horrified pause.)*

EMMA Oh, *dear!*

CHARLES I'm sorry, sir, I thought you were . . . I mean, I hope we haven't disturbed you.

TOM Disturbed me? Nothing to disturb. I wasn't asleep.

EMMA *(to CHARLES)* I'd quite forgotten he was there.

TOM Of course I was there. Where did you think I was? Had my eyes shut, but that's nothing. I can think better with my eyes shut . . *(He rises, and ambles towards the french window)* What's this about you being homeless? You an orphan?

EMMA *(flustered)* Yes, of course, but . . .

TOM *(peering out of the window and talking half to himself)* Pity. We all come to it in time. Do you know, I was only thinking the other day, poor old Lizzie'll be an orphan before so many years. *We* shan't last for ever, can't expect to . . . *(Turning towards EMMA with an airy wave of the hand)* But if you're a homeless orphan, you stay here.

EMMA It's very kind of you, but . . .

(ELIZABETH enters R.)

ELIZABETH Oh, Charles, old Higgins is at the back door. They told him you were here. Will you speak to him?

CHARLES *(rising)* Yes, of course . . . Forgive me. *(He goes out R.)*

ELIZABETH I'm sorry to leave you like this, Emma, but there was still a lot of muddle in the kitchen, and we're clearing up.

EMMA My dear, of course. Can't I help?

ELIZABETH Oh, no thanks. You stay and amuse Father. Shan't be long. *(ELIZABETH goes out R.)*

TOM *(gazing after ELIZABETH and then coming D.R.)* "Stay and amuse Father"—what does the girl mean by that, eh?

EMMA *(nervously)* I expect she only meant we might—well—have a little chat, you know.

TOM Oh. Is that all? Pity . . . *(He looks round)* Where is everybody? I thought there were a lot of people here.

EMMA I think they're busy. And I believe Prudence went for a walk in the garden with—with Mr. Todd.

TOM Todd? He's dead. Died years ago.

EMMA *(with a momentary expression of distress)* Yes . . . Yes, I know. I meant Timothy.

TOM Oh, *Timothy*. Why didn't you say so? *(He sits R.)* You know, I like that lad.

EMMA So do I. He seems a very nice boy.

TOM Can't think where he gets it from. I mean, look at his mother.

Maud seems to *like* Bertha. I don't like Bertha much. Never
did. Too like a horse, don't you think?

EMMA I . . . I really don't know her well. I only met her this
afternoon.

TOM Well, you can *see*, can't you? . . . And Todd—he's dead, of
course, but still, no harm in talking among friends. The boy's
the spit of him to look at, but *he's* got guts. Todd hadn't any
guts. He drank, you know.

EMMA *(in a low voice)* Yes, I know.

TOM *How* do you know? He wasn't at the party. He's . . .

EMMA *(confused)* No, of course he wasn't. I didn't mean . . . I
wasn't thinking.

TOM You *should* think. People don't think enough, that's the
trouble. Todd didn't think, before he married a horse. Mind
you, she kept him in order. She was a bit long in the tooth when
she married him, but perhaps it was good thing. No use marrying
a *nice* woman if you're going to get drunk.
(EMMA gives a little sigh and passes her hand over her eyes.)
I say, are you feeling all right?

EMMA *(recovering herself)* I'm quite all right, thank you. I think
I'm a little . . . cocktails, you know. I'm not used to them.

TOM *(rising)* Have a drink.

EMMA No, *thank* you.

TOM Well, have something . . . *(He looks round for inspiration)*
Have a cigarette.

EMMA I . . . Yes, I think I *will* have a cigarette, thank you.

TOM Good. I'll have one, too. *(He fetches the box from the
bookcase U.R., offers it to EMMA, and takes one himself)* Beastly
things. Generally smoke a pipe, you know. You ever tried a
pipe instead? You should . . . *(He takes the box back to the
bookcase, looks for the matches and, failing to find them, takes
a box from his pocket and lights his own cigarette, but omits
to light EMMA's. He then sits R. again slowly and deliberately,
and looks at EMMA as if he had just noticed her)* I say, have I
seen you before?

EMMA *(rather startled)* Before?

TOM Before you suddenly turned up today, I mean.

EMMA Oh . . . Well, not for a very long time, I'm afraid. I was
a bridesmaid at your wedding, but I don't suppose you even
noticed me.

TOM Don't you believe it. Always had an eye for a pretty girl.
There was one damn pretty bridesmaid, I remember. Not
Bertha—she looked like a horse, still does—another fair-haired
little thing with nice eyes. Was that you?

EMMA I'm afraid not. I was only a small child then. Marjorie
Blessington and I were the *little* bridesmaids.

TOM Oh, yes, there were two brats as well. Can't remember much

28

about them . . . One of them nearly lost her pants in the middle of the service.

EMMA Yes, I . . . remember. You know, although it's so long ago, I remember your wedding perfectly—perhaps because it was the most exciting day I ever had . . . You kissed me.

TOM I—*what?*

EMMA You kissed me. You kissed all the bridesmaids.

TOM All of them? Nonsense. Bertha was a bridesmaid.

EMMA Yes, I know. Any way, when you kissed me, I thought it was *wonderful*. You seemed so romantic and handsome.

TOM *(pleased)* I say . . . was I ?

EMMA *(laughing)* I fell passionately in love with you on the spot.

TOM *(even more pleased)* Did you really? . . . How old did you say you were then?

EMMA Ten.

TOM Oh . . . Oh, well, it's a long time ago now. What have you been doing since? Where do you live?

EMMA Well, at the moment . . .

TOM Oh, yes, I remember. You were telling that parson fellow— whatsisname—Charles. They turned you out, and you're going to stay here. Good. I like you.

EMMA Oh . . Thank you . . That's—that's very kind of you.

TOM Yes, it is. Don't like everybody. Don't like Bertha much . . . What are you fiddling with that cigarette for?

EMMA I—I'm afraid I haven't got a light.

TOM Oh. Why didn't you say so? *(He rises, feels in his pocket for matches, and lights her cigarette.* EMMA *yawns.)* You tired?

EMMA I think I am, a little. It's been an exciting day.

TOM Better go to bed, then. I'm going to bed myself. You're sleeping here, aren't you? I expect there's a bed.

EMMA Oh, yes, Elizabeth's given me a lovely room. There's just one thing—do you think I could borrow a book to read?

TOM A book? Oh, yes, I expect we've got one. *(He goes to the bookcase U.R. and* EMMA *rises and follows him)* What do you want? Scott . . . There's a lot of Scott here.

EMMA I'm afraid I'm not very good at Scott. Have you . . .

TOM *(taking out a volume)* Now, that's a good book. " Life of Gladstone."

EMMA Well . . .

TOM Not much of this modern stuff, I'm afraid. *(Looking at her accusingly)* I expect you like murder.

EMMA Oh, no, indeed. As a matter of fact, I have rather old-fashioned tastes. Have you any of Anthony Trollope? " Barchester Towers " or—or " The Small House at Allington "?

TOM Oh, yes, Trollope. Used to like him myself. You're a sensible girl. Now, let's see.

*(*TOM *and* EMMA *look along the shelves together.*   They are in a*

comfortable huddle, with TOM'S *arm unconsciously round* EMMA'S *shoulder, when* MAUD *and* BERTHA *enter R.)*

MAUD   Tom!

TOM   *(without looking round)*   Eh?
   *(*EMMA *breaks away L., and puffs in an embarrassed manner at her cigarette.)*

MAUD   What *are* you doing?

TOM   I'm looking for some Trollopes.

MAUD   For *what?*

TOM   This girl wants either " Barchester Towers " or " The Small House." Then we're going to bed.

EMMA   Oh, no, not yet . . . I mean, I shouldn't dream of going to bed yet, while you have visitors.

TOM   *(turning and looking round)*   Visitors? . . . Oh, you needn't worry about Bertha. She's always here. Practically lives here.
   *(*ELIZABETH *enters R.)*

ELIZABETH   Who practically lives here?

MAUD   Nobody. Your father's being very rude, as usual. But it's funny you should say that, because it's just what Bertha and I have been talking about. Sit down, Bertha. *(*MAUD *sits C.,* BERTHA *sits R. and* ELIZABETH *goes to collect the coffee cups from the table U.L.)* Did you know that Charles is going to be Vicar of a coal mine in Northamptonshire?

BERTHA   Nottinghamshire.

MAUD   Oh, well, it's much the same thing. Any way, when he goes, Bertha is going to find a little house for herself somewhere here. Won't that be nice?

TOM   Will it?

MAUD   And we thought, until she finds just what she wants, she had better come and live here with us.

TOM   Why?

BERTHA   Only for the time being, of course. Must have my own place as soon as possible; but it would give me a bit more time to look round. It's very decent of Maud to suggest it.

MAUD   Oh, you mustn't give me the credit, dear, it was your idea. But of course, it'll be no trouble. There's plenty of room for you both.

ELIZABETH   *(pausing behind* MAUD'S *chair, with the coffee tray in her hands)*   Both?

BERTHA   She means Timothy as well. He may get a job locally— but that won't be till after next term, and I may be settled by Christmas. *Anything* might happen.

ELIZABETH   *(slowly)*   Yes . . . Yes, it might. *(*ELIZABETH *goes out R. with the coffee tray.)*

BERTHA   I hope Elizabeth doesn't think we're going to butt in and make extra work for her. She sounded a bit . . well. . . .

MAUD   Nonsense. Surely I can ask my friends to stay without consulting my children . . . Tom, it's time you went to bed. I know Bertha will excuse you.

BERTHA *(rising)* As a matter of fact, I think we'd better be pushing off now, in any case. Getting late. *(*ELIZABETH *and* SALLY *enter R.)* Where's Charles?

ELIZABETH Higgins came to fetch him. I think poor old Mrs. Higgins is dying again. I haven't seen Timothy.

EMMA He went into the garden, I think.

BERTHA What, again? Oh, well, I'd better go without him. Send him home when you want to get rid of him, Maud. Goodbye, Elizabeth. 'Bye, Sally. Oh, good night, Er . . . *(to* EMMA.*)*

MAUD *(rising)* All right, Bertha dear, if you really must go, I'll see you out. Tom, it's time you went to bed.

TOM I'm *going* to bed. So's this girl. Oh, and she's going to stay here.

MAUD Of course. I asked her to stay.

TOM Oh, did you? So did I. She's an orphan—aren't you? She's going to stay as long as she likes.

EMMA Oh, no, really, I . . . .

MAUD I myself invited Emma to stay for *(meaningly)* a day or two. Don't interfere, Tom.

TOM Yes, but . . .

MAUD Go to *bed!* *(*MAUD *and* BERTHA *go out R., but as* TOM *lingers* MAUD *comes back)* Tom!

TOM All right, all right. What about this girl? She's tired.

EMMA Oh, no, I'm not in the least tired. I'll stay a little longer. *(She sits L. on the sofa.)*

MAUD *Tom!*

TOM All *right.* *(To* EMMA*)* Good night, m'dear. *(*TOM *and* MAUD *go out R.* ELIZABETH *sits R. and* SALLY *perches on the arm of her chair.)*

SALLY *(to* EMMA*)* Well, of all things! You've got off good and proper with Grandpa. Grannie's green with jealousy.

EMMA Oh, my dear, you mustn't say such things.

SALLY But I think it's lovely. He's such an old pet, and Grannie does nag him so. Why shouldn't he have his fun?

EMMA My dear, I do assure you, there was no question of . . .

SALLY *(rising and crossing to L. to sit beside* EMMA*)* Besides, I'm glad he likes you. We like you, too. Aunt Liz and I were talking about you in the kitchen.

ELIZABETH Sally, stop it.

SALLY Emma doesn't mind. I say, *can* I call you Emma?

EMMA Of course you can.

SALLY Good. Well, the thing is, we're bursting with curiosity about what you said to Timothy this morning.

ELIZABETH We're nothing of the sort. Be quiet, Sally.

SALLY Well, I am, any way; and you were frightfully intrigued when I told you, you know you were, Aunt Liz . . . Emma, do tell us, what did you mean about Timothy being like his father? Did you know him—Timothy's father, I mean?

EMMA   Yes . . . Yes, I knew him.

SALLY   When you were young?

EMMA   When I was young.   When I was about your age, in fact.

SALLY   I *say!*   Was he a boy friend of yours?

ELIZABETH   That will do, Sally.   *(She gets up, wanders listlessly to the bookcase and then to the french window, obviously restless and nervy.)*

EMMA   No, I should like to tell you about it.   I think perhaps I'd rather you didn't tell Timothy—or—or his mother.

SALLY   *That* old trout?   Rather not.   We won't tell a soul, I promise . .   Were you in love with him?

EMMA   I was enaged to him.

SALLY   *Oh!* . . . What happened?   Did he chuck you?

EMMA   No, I chucked . . . I mean, I broke off the engagement.   It hadn't been announced, and nobody knew except my mother.

SALLY   Did *she* make you break it off?   How mean.

EMMA   No, not really.   There were . . . several reasons.   And my mother needed me.

SALLY   I see . . . Did you mind *awfully?*

EMMA   I minded very much at the time.   One gets over these things, you know.

SALLY   Does one?   I don't think I should.   Would you, Aunt Liz?

ELIZABETH   *(absentmindedly)*   What?

SALLY   Oh, you're not listening.   You've no soul, Aunt Liz. Here's a real-life romance under your very nose and you're not even interested . . . What I don't understand, you know, Emma, is how any one who had been in love with someone nice like you could have gone off and married an old hag like Bertha.

EMMA   Yes, I know . . . I mean . . . well, any way, my dear, I suppose she wasn't quite such an old hag in those days . . . No, I don't mean that, either, of course.   Oh dear, you're making me quite catty.

SALLY   And quite right, too.   I should be catty if I'd had my life blighted like that.

EMMA   Oh, good gracious, my life isn't in the least blighted.   I've been very happy.   I confess it was a shock this morning, seeing Timothy suddenly like that; but really it's all over and done with. I do admit one thing, though I dare say it's very wrong of me . . .

SALLY   What?

EMMA   Somehow—I don't know what it is—but I don't feel I could ever really *like* Bertha.

(PRUDENCE and TIMOTHY enter through the french window. PRUDENCE gives ELIZABETH a self-satisfied smile, which ELIZABETH greets with a stony stare.)

PRUDENCE Hello. Where's everybody?

ELIZABETH *(shortly)* Gone to bed.

PRUDENCE Oh, is it as late as all that? I didn't realise we'd been out so long. The time's gone very quickly, hasn't it, Timothy?

TIMOTHY *(uncomfortably)* Er—yes.

PRUDENCE We found so much to talk about. *(She yawns)* I think I'll push off now, if nobody minds.

ELIZABETH I don't suppose anybody minds.

PRUDENCE You'll forgive me, won't you, Timothy? You're—almost one of the family. Good night, my dear. It's been a lovely talk.

(PRUDENCE takes TIMOTHY's hands for a moment, and then makes her exit R. There is an uncomfortable pause.)

EMMA } *(together)* I think if you don't mind . . .
TIMOTHY } Well, I suppose I'd better . . .

EMMA I beg your pardon.

TIMOTHY Sorry.

EMMA *(rising)* I was only going to say, I think if you don't mind I'll go to bed, too. I've had *such* an exciting day.

ELIZABETH Yes, of course. I'll come up with you.

TIMOTHY I must go, too.

ELIZABETH Don't hurry. As Prudence says, you're one of the family.

EMMA *(going with ELIZABETH towards the door R.)* Good night, Sally.

SALLY Good night. Sleep well.

EMMA *(turning diffidently to TIMOTHY)* Good night . . . Timothy.

TIMOTHY Oh—er—good night.

(ELIZABETH and EMMA go out R. There is a slight pause, as TIMOTHY hovers uncertainly, as if wondering whether he ought to go too, and SALLY curls up on the sofa L. and looks at him with sardonic amusement.)

SALLY My poor, poor Timothy.

TIMOTHY *(turning sharply towards her)* Eh?

SALLY Mummie's latest victim.

TIMOTHY What the devil are you talking about?

SALLY Well, don't say I didn't warn you. *I* know Mummie, and I know her methods . . . What did you talk about in the garden?

TIMOTHY *(sitting on arm of chair R.)* Oh, I don't know—this and that. I think we talked chiefly about your mother's own affairs.

SALLY I bet you did. Did she mention about being misunderstood?

TIMOTHY *(startled)* Well, she . . .

SALLY *(sitting up and speaking dramatically)* And all her life she'd been searching for something she'd never managed to find? Underneath a calm and composed exterior was a heart craving for real affection and understanding?

TIMOTHY Look here, were you listening?

SALLY *(relaxing again)* Not this time. Actually, I don't nowadays. I used to. Once, when I was a kid, I climbed a tree in the garden and heard the whole thing from start to finish—or very nearly. They were sitting underneath.

TIMOTHY They?

SALLY Mummie and her current boy friend. It was the most consecutive performance I've ever managed; and even then I fell out just before the curtain line.

TIMOTHY *(rising and moving C. behind chair)* Sally, what are you up to? Are you trying to tell me that Prudence makes a habit of talking about herself like she—well, like—er . . .

SALLY Like she did to you tonight? Well, of course she does. She's an awful idiot in some ways.

TIMOTHY *(virtuously)* You're not to talk about your mother like that. *(He returns to the chair R. and sits.)*

SALLY I mean, it's so unoriginal. You'd think she'd been reading " Poppy's Paper " or something. The funny thing is they all seem to fall for it.

TIMOTHY All?

SALLY All the poor, unsuspecting males she tries to ensnare. I could understand the old ones, because they fall for anything; but it seems to go down with the comparatively young ones like you, too.

TIMOTHY I think you're talking an awful lot of rot, my child. I've known your mother for a considerable number of years, and why she should suddenly want to ensnare me, as you call it, I can't imagine.

SALLY *(slowly)* No . . No, that's the funny thing. If you were married, or even engaged, I could understand it. She generally concentrates on someone else's property.

TIMOTHY Sally, that's a beastly thing to say. Stop it.

SALLY You're not married, are you?

TIMOTHY Certainly not.

SALLY Or engaged?

TIMOTHY *No.*

SALLY Oh . . . *(She considers for a moment)* You're not thinking of getting engaged? I mean, are you Paying Attention to anyone in particular?

TIMOTHY What a revolting expression.

SALLY I know—isn't it heavenly? I got it from my old Nannie . . . . *Are* you?

TIMOTHY Am I what?

SALLY Paying Attention to anyone?

TIMOTHY No, of course not.

SALLY I just wondered. I'm only trying to analyse Mummie's motives. If she suspects you're keen on someone, it's quite enough to make her behave as she did tonight. She can't help it—it's a sort of Thing she's got. I expect she needs psycho-analysing or something.

TIMOTHY *(rising and going towards door R.)* *You* need your bottom smacked. Good night.

SALLY No, don't go. I want to sort this out. Timothy . . .

TIMOTHY *(turning)* Well?

SALLY I've been thinking.

TIMOTHY I'm glad to hear it. Good night. *(He makes as if to go again.)*

SALLY Does Mummie think there's something between you and Aunt Liz?

(A pause, as TIMOTHY *hesitates, and then turns back towards* SALLY*.)*

TIMOTHY *(as off-handedly as possible)* What put that idea into your head?

SALLY I don't quite know . . . Yes, I do. It was the way Mummie looked at Aunt Liz when you came in from the garden just now —a sort of . . . of *triumphant* look . . . Oh, Timothy, sit down a minute. *(*TIMOTHY *hesitates, and then sits reluctantly C.)* I know I've been joking about Mummie's antics, but I'm serious now. I don't mind so much when it's people I hardly know, but when she does it to someone I'm fond of it's different. If she's trying to make Aunt Liz unhappy, I'll be furious.

TIMOTHY You needn't worry.

SALLY How do *you* know? I suppose she's a bit old for you, but if that doesn't worry Mummie I don't see why it should worry Aunt Liz. For all you know, she may have a terrific secret passion for you. I believe women of her age get all sorts of funny ideas.

TIMOTHY I can assure you that your aunt has no funny ideas about me at all.

SALLY *(earnestly)* I don't see how you can be sure. Aunt Liz doesn't show her feelings—you never know quite what she's thinking . . . *(She sits up suddenly)* Unless of course you've *asked* her? Have you?

TIMOTHY Mind your own business.

SALLY *(springing to her feet)* Oh! Does that mean you have? Have you really?

TIMOTHY Blast you! Yes, I have. Now are you satisfied?

SALLY You mean you've really asked Aunt Liz to marry you? And she turned you down?

TIMOTHY Quite definitely.

SALLY *(easing L.)* Oh, what a pity. I should have liked you for an uncle . . . But I wonder how Mummie knew that?

TIMOTHY *(rising and moving R.)* I don't suppose she did know, unless she has second sight—like her daughter. All I'm trying to tell you is that Elizabeth has no—er—interest in me at all, and you needn't worry about Prudence making her unhappy. Now you know, and you can keep it to yourself, if you don't mind.

SALLY *(sitting on arm of sofa)* Of course I will. What do you take me for? Oh dear, now I'm quite worried about *you* instead.

TIMOTHY Thank you. You needn't be.

SALLY Aren't you heartbroken? Aren't you going out into the Great Open Spaces, where men are men . . . ?

TIMOTHY No, I'm not. I'm going back to the Vicarage, where my Mamma has probably locked me out.

SALLY *(thoughtfully)* You know, you don't sound as if you were heartbroken.

TIMOTHY *(turning and coming C.)* What do you mean?

SALLY I don't know, quite. I think I mean that, if you'd really minded, you wouldn't have told me.

TIMOTHY *(after a pause)* Do you know, I think you're right.

SALLY I often am. Nobody gives me credit for it, but beneath a—a youthful and frivolous exterior I have great per-spi-ca-ci-ty . . . *That's* a good word.

TIMOTHY You're a precocious infant, but I'm afraid you *are* right. I've been wondering why, at the back of my mind, I've been feeling almost—relieved. I was rather shattered at first.

SALLY *(with an air of great wisdom)* I expect you took too much for granted, and your vanity was hurt.

TIMOTHY Possibly—blast you! The funny thing is, I'd been screwing up my courage to ask her for months—years, almost— and then, when I got it out at last, she said something which made me think.

SALLY What?

TIMOTHY She said: " It's very kind of you to be sorry for me. Is that why you're asking me to marry you?

SALLY Oh, I see. You mean she thought you were just taking pity on her—Pity is Akin to Love, and that sort of thing.

TIMOTHY Something like that . . . I denied it at the time, of course.

SALLY Of course.

TIMOTHY But, thinking it over, I believe she was right. It's made me feel rather ashamed of myself . . . Look here, why am I saying all this to a chit like you?

SALLY *(trying to look smug)* Because I'm so sympathetic and understanding.

TIMOTHY Because you talk too much, and the habit's catching. But as long as you keep it to yourself, there's no harm done.

SALLY *(rising)* I told you I would. I don't betray confidences. Can I give you a piece of advice?

TIMOTHY *(indignantly)* Certainly not.

SALLY *(going up to him)* All right, I will. You should never, never be *sorry* for people—especially when they deserve it. They don't like it.

TIMOTHY *(taking her hands)* You're a funny kid, but you're rather sweet.

36

(MAUD and ELIZABETH enter R. and TIMOTHY and SALLY break away from each other.)

MAUD Oh, Timothy, are you still here?

TIMOTHY Sorry. I was just going. *(He moves towards the door R.)*

SALLY *(in Nanny-like tones)* Come, come, de-ar. Haven't we forgotten something?

TIMOTHY *(turning)* What are you talking about?

SALLY What do we say when we've had a lovely party?

TIMOTHY *(without rancour)* What a revolting child you are . . . *(To MAUD)* I'm so sorry—Good night, and . . . thank-you-very-much-for-having-me. *(He makes a face at SALLY)* Good night, Sally. *(A slight pause)* Good night—Liz. *(TIMOTHY goes out R.)*

SALLY *(sitting on the arm of the chair C.)* He's really rather a poppet.

MAUD Who, dear?

SALLY Timothy. It's funny—I suppose he must be getting on a bit, actually, but he seems so *young*. I used to think of him as a sort of uncle. *(She suddenly realises the possible implications of this remark, and glances guiltily at ELIZABETH.)*

MAUD *(vaguely)* I don't think he can be, dear, he's an only child. It's time you went to bed. Run along, there's a good girl.

SALLY *(with mock meekness)* Yes, Grandmamma. And-don't-forget-to-brush-your-teeth-and-say-your-prayers . . Darling, Gran, *(rising and kissing MAUD)* when will you stop treating me as if I were about six? Good-night, Aunt Liz. It's time you went to bed, too. You look tired to death. 'Night, Gran. *(SALLY goes out R.)*

MAUD I think we're all tired. I am myself, but I try not to show it. I'm glad the party went so well. *(She moves vaguely round, plumping cushions and making a show of tidying up, while ELIZABETH for once stands idly U.R. fiddling with an ash tray.)*

ELIZABETH Yes.

MAUD I think everybody enjoyed it. It was a lot of trouble, of course, but I don't mind that for once in a way.

ELIZABETH No.

MAUD I think your father got rather over-excited. He was behaving in the most extraordinary way before he went to bed.

ELIZABETH Was he?

MAUD *(turning and looking at ELIZABETH)* Elizabeth, are you listening to a word I say?

ELIZABETH No . . . I mean yes. Yes, of course I'm listening.

MAUD *(sharply)* Elizabeth!

ELIZABETH *(coming down R.)* Oh, I'm sorry, Mother. I'm just rather tired, that's all.

MAUD Well, really, my dear, it's time you pulled yourself together and learned to control your feelings. You've been in a most tiresome mood all day.

ELIZABETH *(wearily)* I'm sorry.

MAUD I should hope so. It's so selfish, and today of all days. It's very nice for you, being the only daughter at home, but you can't have it all your own way *all* the time.

ELIZABETH No, I can't, can I?

MAUD I suppose you're annoyed now because I've asked Bertha to stay for a little while. You don't seem to realise that I should like the company of my own generation once in a way.

ELIZABETH *(under her breath)* So should I.

MAUD What did you say? What do you mean?

ELIZABETH *(suddenly giving way)* I mean I'm sick, sorry and tired of everything and everybody. I'm tired of being talked to as if I were a schoolgirl instead of a middle-aged woman . . .

MAUD Middle-aged? What nonsense. Of course you're not middle . . .

ELIZABETH And I'm tired of being a doormat, and I'm tired of being tied up here and never able to get away, and I'm tired of—of—well, any way *(suddenly calming down and sitting R.)* I'm just tired, that's all.

MAUD *(coldly)* I think you'd better go to bed.

ELIZABETH Yes, I'd better.

MAUD I can't think what's made you so hysterical. What on earth do you *want?*

ELIZABETH I want to—go away.

MAUD Go *away?* But—but you can't.

ELIZABETH No, I can't.

MAUD Of course you can't. Why, this is your home.

ELIZABETH Yes, I know.

MAUD You couldn't go away, and leave me and your father after all these years. We're not as young as we were, my dear, surely you must realise that.

ELIZABETH I do realise it.

MAUD Well, I'm glad you do. Perhaps you're a little run down, and a change would do you good. You haven't had a holiday for some time . . .

ELIZABETH About twelve years.

MAUD And I've just had an idea. Perhaps when Bertha's here she might help me with the housekeeping for a week or two, and we could spare you to go and stay with Prudence or something.

ELIZABETH Or something.

MAUD What did you say?

ELIZABETH Nothing.

MAUD *(doubtfully)* Oh . . . Well, even if you said nothing, don't say it under your breath like that, dear. It's very rude, and Mother doesn't like it. I'm doing my best to be sympathetic, and I dare say you're a little overwrought, but . . .

(TOM, clad in dressing gown and pyjamas, rushes in R.)

TOM (*coming C. behind chair*) I say, can you *do* something? That girl's passed out.

MAUD Passed out? What are you talking about, Tom?

TOM That girl. She's fainted.

ELIZABETH (*rising*) Sally? Oh, surely not.

TOM No, no, that's not her name. What-do-you-call-her—the Emma one.

MAUD Emma's fainted? How very tiresome. How?

TOM What do you mean, how? *I* don't know. I haven't fainted. I don't faint. It's that girl. She . . .

ELIZABETH (*going towards door R.*) I'd better go and see what it's all about. (*She turns to* TOM) Where is she? In her room?

TOM Of course she isn't in her room. How should I know, if she'd fainted in her room? She's passed out flat on the floor of my dressing-room, blast it.

(ELIZABETH *goes out R.*)

MAUD (*returning to her inept efforts to tidy cushions on the sofa L.*) You'd better go back to bed, Tom.

TOM I haven't *been* to bed yet. I'm not ready for bed.

MAUD (*with her back to him*) Well, go back and *get* ready.

TOM I can't. How can I get ready for bed when there's a body all over the floor of my dressing-room?

MAUD (*suddenly realising, and turning to* TOM) Tom! What was Emma *doing* in your dressing-room?

TOM Doing? *She* wasn't doing anything. I asked her in.

MAUD You *asked* her in?

TOM I met her on the landing on the way to the . . . Well, I saw her on the landing and I asked her in.

MAUD (*awfully*) Why?

TOM Why? Because I'd just remembered, I used to keep some Trollopes there. We were looking for them, when she suddenly went *wallop* and passed out . . . Most extraordinary . . . I say, Maud, I like that girl.

MAUD (*coldly*) Evidently.

TOM She's got sense. She listens to what you say.

MAUD I suppose you mean she listens to what *you* say.

TOM Yes, that's what I mean. Women don't listen as a rule. Look at your pal Bertha. Talks the hind leg off a donkey if you give her a chance, but she never *listens.* Look at Prudence. Look at Lizzie, even . . .

MAUD (*dangerously*) And look at *me*, I suppose?

TOM Yes, exactly. (MAUD *sits L. and burst into tears*) Good God, Maudie, what the hell's the matter?

MAUD Don't swear at me!

TOM (*moving to behind sofa and leaning over* MAUD) Swear at you? I'm not swearing at you. I simply asked you what the bloody hell's the matter? Why, it's years since I saw you blubber like that.

MAUD It's—years—since—I . . . since I saw you *behave* like that.

TOM Like what?

MAUD M-making a fool of yourself over a woman.

TOM *(looking round)* What woman?

MAUD *(wailing)* Oh-oh-oooh!

TOM *(moving C.)* I wish I knew what you were talking about.

MAUD You know perfectly well what I'm talking about. First you behave in a—in a most *abandoned* way with a woman you hardly know, and then you insult me and tell me I neglect you.

TOM Who said you neglected me? I didn't. I said . . .

MAUD You said I never listened to you.

TOM *(helplessly)* Well, you don't, do you?

MAUD First Elizabeth and then you. I'm obviously a nuisance to everyone. It's time I was dead.

TOM Oh, no, Maudie, I wouldn't say that . . . Any way, what's Lizzie got to do with it?

MAUD *(wiping her eyes)* Just before you came down just now, Elizabeth was talking in the *wildest* way, and threatening to leave home.

TOM Leave home? What for?

MAUD What for, indeed? That's what *I* want to know. You're so selfish, I told her . . .

TOM Oh, come, Maudie, that's not fair. Nobody could call Lizzie selfish. She's not like Prudence. Prudence takes after you. But . . .

MAUD *(tensely)* What did you say?

TOM *(blankly)* I don't know. What did I say? I've forgotten.

MAUD *(bursting into fresh tears)* How can you?

TOM How can I what?

MAUD Call me selfish.

TOM Did I? Well, but you are, aren't you? Nothing in that. Always have been.

MAUD Oh-oh-oooh!

TOM Well, I mean, you like your own way, and all that.

MAUD *(pettishly)* I don't like my own way.

TOM Oh, don't you? I'm sorry about that, Maudie, I thought you did.

MAUD What makes you think I like my own way?

TOM *(at loss)* Well, I dunno . . . I suppose I mean—bossing everyone about, and—and . . .

MAUD And what?

TOM Oh, telling everyone what to do, if you know what I mean. Just saying what *you* want—not asking them, I mean. Not . . . Oh, I dunno . . . What are we talking about?

MAUD We seem to be talking about my shortcomings.

TOM *(moving to MAUD and patting her on the shoulder)* Your short-comings? Nonsense, Maudie, you haven't got any shortcomings.

MAUD   Except that I don't listen to you, and I'm selfish, and I order everyone about, and think of nobody but myself.

TOM   Yes, but . . .

MAUD   If you think so badly of me, I can't think why you've taken fifty years to tell me so.

TOM   Good God, I don't think badly of you.   What gave you that idea?   I only said . . .

MAUD   You only said I was selfish, and a few other things as well.   Why haven't you told me all this before?

TOM   I don't think you ever asked me.

MAUD   *Asked* you?

TOM   I suppose I thought you knew . . . I mean, I suppose I just thought you liked it that way, and . . .
      (ELIZABETH enters R.)

ELIZABETH   I think she's all right now.

TOM   Who?

ELIZABETH   Emma, of course.

TOM   Oh . . . *(He thinks this over)*   Wasn't she all right before?

ELIZABETH *(patiently)*   She fainted, *dear* Father, in your dressing-room, you may remember.   Actually, she'd come to before I got upstairs, and was back in her own room.

TOM   Fainted, did she?   What's the matter with her?

ELIZABETH   She seems to attribute it to cocktails, but I think myself she's overtired, and a bit het up about something.   I'll get the doctor to look at her in the morning if she isn't better.   Mother, how long did you ask her to stay for?

MAUD *(absentmindedly)*   What? . . . I don't remember.

ELIZABETH   Personally, I think what she needs is a good rest.   If she can manage it, I wondered whether . . . *(hesitatingly)* . . . whether we might suggest her staying on here for a bit.   What do you think?

TOM   Yes.   Good idea.

ELIZABETH   Don't be tactless, Father . . . Mother, do you think . . . ?

MAUD *(with beautiful resignation)*   I leave it entirely to you, dear.

ELIZABETH *(taken aback)*   Oh . . . Oh, well, I'll see what she says in the morning.   Father, aren't you going to bed?

TOM   Of course I'm going to bed.   Can't think what you called me down for.   *(He goes towards the door R.)*   Don't sit up late yourself, Maudie.
      (TOM goes out R.   MAUD sits looking straight before her, deep in thought.)

ELIZABETH *(looking at her curiously)*   Are you feeling all right, Mother?

MAUD   What? . . . Oh, yes, quite all right, thank you, dear.   Don't worry about me at *all*.

ELIZABETH *(crossing L. to MAUD and kneeling in front of her)*   Mother, are you sure you're all right?   What's the matter?

MAUD   Nothing . . . Nothing, really.   I was just wishing . . .
ELIZABETH   What?
MAUD   Elizabeth, I've been married to your father for fifty years . . .
ELIZABETH   Yes.   Well?
MAUD   And I *still* wish . . . I do so wish . . . that he wouldn't always call me *"Maudie"*!

CURTAIN

ACT III
Morning a fortnight later.

When the curtain goes up, TIMOTHY *and* SALLY *are standing slightly R.C. in close embrace.* ELIZABETH *appears at the french window with a bunch of flowers in her hand. She sees them, reacts, and hesitates.* SALLY *catches sight of her, breaks away, and makes for the door R.)*

TIMOTHY Here, I say, Sally . . .

SALLY You tell her.

*(*SALLY *goes out quickly R.* ELIZABETH *enters, glances at* TIMOTHY, *and turns her back as she arranges the flowers on the table U.L.* TIMOTHY *looks sheepish, and there is a pause.)*

ELIZABETH *(at last, conversationally)* I—er—didn't know you were here, Timothy. Good morning.

TIMOTHY What?

ELIZABETH I said "Good morning." That's all.

TIMOTHY Oh . . . Yes, it is, isn't it?

ELIZABETH It is what?

TIMOTHY A good morning.

ELIZABETH Oh.

TIMOTHY *(wandering to the cigarette box U.R. and helping himself)* It was—er—a lovely morning, and I thought I could do with a walk, so I—er—came for a walk. I—er—just walked up here.

ELIZABETH *(busy with the flowers)* You know we're always glad to see you. Sit down somewhere. Have a cigarette.

TIMOTHY *(lighting it)* Thanks. *(He sits on the arm of the chair R.)* How's everyone?

ELIZABETH All right, I think. *(Pointedly)* Much the same as they were when you were here yesterday, and the day before, and the day before that.

TIMOTHY Er—yes . . Good.

ELIZABETH As a matter of fact, Mothers' been a bit *quiet* lately, but I don't think it's anything to worry about.

TIMOTHY Oh. Is she usually noisy?

ELIZABETH No, but . . . she's not quite herself, somehow. I don't quite know what it is. I thought at first she didn't like Emma being here so long, but curiously enough they seem to get on like a house on fire now. Emma helps her with her knitting. She's even been teaching her to tat.

TIMOTHY Old Emma all right again?

ELIZABETH Oh Lord, yes. I think the poor dear was thoroughly overwrought, and had had rather a shock to the system, being turned out like that. She's still fussing a bit about her old Mrs. Robinson, and itching to get back to her, but otherwise she's all right. *(She finishes the flowers and turns round)* In fact, I've come to the conclusion that Emma's very much all right. She's rather a wonder.

43

TIMOTHY   In what way?

ELIZABETH *(coming down C.)* She's got a—a knack with the parents.
Father took a terrific fancy to her straight away, and I thought
that would put Mother off completely; and it did at first.   But
after a few days they were as thick as thieves.   It's funny—you'd
think Emma was as meek as a mouse, and that Mother would
bully her to distraction; and she does in a way.   But Emma lets
it all slide off, and comes up smiling, and in the end she twiddles
Mamma round her little finger without her realising it.   I wish . . .
(She stops.)

TIMOTHY   What do you wish?

ELIZABETH   Nothing . . . At least, I mean I wish I had Emma's gift
in dealing with Mother.   She's my own mother, after all, but I've
never been able to to cope with her like that.

TIMOTHY   Perhaps it's because she *is* your own mother.   One's
own relations are *always* worse than other people's.   I've noticed
it myself.

ELIZABETH   Do you know, that's one of your more intelligent
remarks.   Oh, well . . *(She moves towards him)*   Get out of the
way a minute, the carpet's rucked up under that chair.
*(TIMOTHY rises and moves away L., while ELIZABETH bends down
and straightens the carpet.)*

TIMOTHY   *(after a pause)*   Lizzie . . .

ELIZABETH   Yes?

TIMOTHY   You shoving me round the room like that—does it remind
you of anything?

ELIZABETH   *(busy with the carpet)*   Remind me of anything?

TIMOTHY   Of—another conversation we had a—a short time ago.

ELIZABETH   *(pausing but remaining on her knees)*   Did we?   Now,
which conversation would that be, I wonder?

TIMOTHY   Oh hell!   *(They look at each other for a few moments,
then ELIZABETH relents, smiles at him, and rises.)*

ELIZABETH   All right, Timmy, I'll help you out.   What are you
trying to tell me?   You and Sally?

TIMOTHY   I'm afraid so.

ELIZABETH   What do you mean, you're afraid so?   Not very
gallant, are you?

TIMOTHY   You know what I mean.   You of all people must think
me a bit . . well . . .

ELIZABETH   Changeable?

TIMOTHY   I think the word is " fickle."

ELIZABETH   Well, I don't think so.   You can forget about me.
Are you and Sally engaged?

TIMOTHY   I'm afraid so—I mean, yes, as a matter of fact, we are.

ELIZABETH   I'm very glad to hear it.

TIMOTHY   I say, do you mean that?

ELIZABETH   *(sitting on arm of chair R.)*   I mean I'm glad your
Intentions are Strictly Honourable.   When I came in just now, I

just wondered. I'd rather you didn't play about with Sally's feelings.

TIMOTHY What about *your* feelings? You must think I don't know my own mind.

ELIZABETH Oh, for Heaven's sake! What do you think I am? A dog in the manger? You asked me to marry you, and I refused you. Why should my feelings be hurt because you've discovered I was right, and you'd much rather marry Sally instead?

TIMOTHY Oh, I say, Lizzie, don't put it quite like that.

ELIZABETH Well, wouldn't you?

TIMOTHY Wouldn't I what?

ELIZABETH Rather marry Sally.

TIMOTHY Well, of course, I . . .

ELIZABETH Of course you would, and I'm very, very glad about it, Timmy. You'll suit each other down to the ground.

TIMOTHY I'm much too old for her, of course.

ELIZABETH *(rising and putting a hand on his shoulder)* You'll never be too old for anyone. I don't suppose you'll ever really grow up. Now, you go and find Sally and take her for a walk or something—I'm busy. But the way, have you told Prudence.

TIMOTHY No, not yet. Nobody knows but you.

ELIZABETH Then you'd better.

TIMOTHY Oh, my God. Yes, I suppose I had. How difficult life is.

ELIZABETH I don't see why Prudence should be particularly difficult about it.

TIMOTHY *(going towards door R.)* No, you wouldn't.

*(*TIMOTHY *goes out R.* ELIZABETH *looks after him thoughtfully for a moment or two, wanders back to chair C. and sits on the arm, lost in thought. Then she gives herself a little shake and a shrug, rises and eases L. as* FLORRIE *enters R. with a duster in her hand.)*

FLORRIE Excuse me, Miss Allen.

ELIZABETH *(turning)* What is it, Florrie?

FLORRIE You wouldn't have seen my duster anywhere, would you?

ELIZABETH I don't think so—unless you mean the one in your hand.

FLORRIE What? . . . Oh, there now, aren't I a one? I've been looking for it all over the place. *(She hesitates and lingers.)*

ELIZABETH Florrie, if you wanted an excuse to come in and talk, you might have tried to find a better one.

FLORRIE *(coming down C.)* I did try, but I couldn't think of anything. And I knew you were here alone, so I thought it was a good chance.

ELIZABETH Do you want to see me about something?

FLORRIE *(twisting the duster)* Well, yes *and* no, if you see what I mean.

ELIZABETH I don't.

FLORRIE No, well, I didn't expect you to, really. It's just that . . . . Oh, I don't really know how to tell you.

ELIZABETH *(sitting L.)* All right, I may as well know the worst. I suppose it came in two in your hand. What's the particular damage this time?

FLORRIE *(coming towards* ELIZABETH, *and leaning confidentially over the end of the sofa)* Oh, I wouldn't say it was *damage* exactly. It's me.

ELIZABETH Oh. In what way?

FLORRIE *(coyly)* I'm going to get engaged.

ELIZABETH You're going to . . . ? Oh, Florrie, how nice.

FLORRIE Well, it is rather, isn't it?

ELIZABETH I'm very glad. I'd no idea you were thinking of . . . Who is he? Have you known him long?

FLORRIE Well, yes, quite a bit, off and on, as you might say. It's Kennie's father.

ELIZABETH Oh . . . Oh, yes, I see. How—how nice.

FLORRIE Yes, well, that's what I think. It's all in the family, as you might say. Not like a complete stranger, is it? Mind you, he'd have married me at the time if he'd had to—he was always nice mannered and ever so considerate—but . . . well . . . I don't know. Mum thought I was a bit young then for that sort of thing.

ELIZABETH What—sort of thing?

FLORRIE Getting married.

ELIZABETH Oh.

FLORRIE Then he went away, and we sort of lost touch. What with one thing and another I hadn't seen him for five years, not till he came back here a bit ago.

ELIZABETH I see. Is he living here now?

FLORRIE Oh, yes, he's got a job with Mr. Dawkins at the farm. Mind you, I never think farm work's very refined—look at the cows and everything—but he was brought up to it, so I suppose you don't notice so much. And it means we can live with Mum, if the lodger doesn't mind doubling up a bit.

ELIZABETH Well, I'm very glad you're not going right away, Florrie. I hope you'll manage to go on working here, even when you're married.

FLORRIE *(crossing slowly towards door R.)* Oh, gracious, yes, Miss Allen. Getting married doesn't make any difference to what *I* do. Any way, we shan't be getting married for a bit. Why, we're not getting engaged, even, until next week, and Mum doesn't want us to rush things. Better be safe than sorry, she says.

ELIZABETH Does she? Well, I'm sure she's right. Any way, it's very exciting news.

FLORRIE It's a relief, any way. After all, I'm gone twenty-four, and I was beginning to think I was on the shelf, too. I shouldn't like to be old maid . . . *(She turns, and comes back L. to* ELIZABETH*)* I say, Miss Allen.

ELIZABETH Yes?

FLORRIE Excuse me asking, but being in the same way myself sort of brought it to mind . . . Is there anything between Mr. Todd and Miss Sally?

ELIZABETH Why do you ask that?

FLORRIE Because I wanted to know. I just thought there might be. I sort of thought—well—it'd be ever so exciting if *two* people in the family got engaged together, wouldn't it?

ELIZABETH It would, wouldn't it? Well, we shall have to wait and see.

FLORRIE Ooh, I hope they will. Two weddings—that's sure to mean a third. Now, who could that be?

ELIZABETH I've no ideas at all, I'm afraid.

FLORRIE Oh, go on! It might even be you.

ELIZABETH *(rising)* Very unlikely, I think. Now, if you don't mind, Florrie . . .

FLORRIE *(drifting towards the door R. again)* Well, yes, it is, but you never know. After all, I had an auntie who wasn't married till she was close on forty—and then, would you believe it, she wore a white dress and everything. It didn't seem quite decent to me . . . *(She pauses and turns)* Miss Allen, that's what I've been wondering about.

ELIZABETH What now?

FLORRIE If you was me, would you be married in white? Mum seems to fancy me in scarlet.

(BERTHA enters through the french window. She looks at FLORRIE, who for once seems to take a hint, and goes out R., humming carelessly to herself.)

BERTHA *(advancing down C.)* Does that girl ever do any work?

ELIZABETH Florrie? Oh, yes, sometimes. How are you, Bertha? *(She indicates the chair C. and sits herself L. again on sofa.)*

BERTHA *(sitting C.)* Bloody cross.

ELIZABETH Oh. What about?

BERTHA I've had all my plans mucked about.

ELIZABETH What plans?

BERTHA What plans? You may well ask. I move Heaven and earth to find a house and make a home for Timothy . . .

ELIZABETH Oh, have you found a house already? I didn't know.

BERTHA Of course I haven't found a house *yet*. I haven't started to look—give me time. But I get it all worked out, and then what happens?

ELIZABETH Timothy says he's going to get married instead.

BERTHA Exactly—mucks up everything, and I shall have to think again. Damn nuisance . . . Here, what do *you* know about it? I met them only a minute ago, and I gathered they'd only just fixed it up.

ELIZABETH I think they had. I rather think I interrupted the actual fixing-up process, so they more or less had to tell me.

Aren't you pleased?

BERTHA Haven't had time to be pleased. I'm bloody cross.

ELIZABETH Yes, so you said. But apart from your own plans being upset, what about Timothy? And Sally? You like Sally, don't you?

BERTHA Of course I like Sally.

ELIZABETH Well, then.

BERTHA Can't think what Timothy wants to get married *for*.

ELIZABETH The usual reasons, I expect.

BERTHA Never known him want to do such a thing before. Oh well, I suppose I shall have to think again. It's a bit hard. First Charles breaks up my home by rushing off to some uncivilised place that no one's ever heard of; and then, when I get it all worked out, Timothy goes and alters everything again. What a life!

(CHARLES *appears at the french window.*)

CHARLES May I come in?

ELIZABETH Oh, hello. Yes, do come in. Bertha's here.

CHARLES *(coming down C. between* BERTHA *and* ELIZABETH) So I see. You look a bit worried, Aunt Bertha. What's the matter?

BERTHA I'm bl . . . I'm annoyed.

CHARLES Oh dear. With me?

BERTHA With both of you.

CHARLES Both? Who's the other one? And what have I done?

BERTHA First you desert me and go off to some God-forsaken place . . .

CHARLES *(mildly)* Not God-forsaken, I hope, Aunt Bertha. I believe even the Midlands are reasonably . . .

BERTHA And then Timothy goes off and gets married.

CHARLES Oh, has he? When?

ELIZABETH He hasn't—yet. He's engaged to Sally.

CHARLES Oh, that.

BERTHA *(looking at him fiercely)* Did you know?

CHARLES Well, not definitely, but I rather thought I saw it coming in the last few days. I'm glad they've fixed it up.

BERTHA Pah!

CHARLES What did you say?

BERTHA I said—" Pah! "

CHARLES Yes, I thought you did. How extraordinary. I've never actually *heard* anyone say it before . . Any way, why " Pah "?

BERTHA Because it upsets all my plans. Because I was all set to find a house and make a home for my son, and now there's no point. They needn't think I'm going to live with *them*, because nothing would persuade me to.

CHARLES Good.

BERTHA What did you say?

CHARLES Nothing . . But any way, Aunt Bertha, is there any reason why you shouldn't go ahead and find a house just the same—for yourself, I mean.

BERTHA *(gloomily)* Not the same incentive. *I* don't know. I'm beginning to think I may as well come with you, after all.

CHARLES *(anxiously)* You mean—to Nottinghamshire.

BERTHA Well, that's where you're going, isn't it.?

CHARLES *(with a desperate glance at* ELIZABETH*)* Er—yes. Of course. Thank you very much, Aunt Bertha, for thinking of it. It's very kind of you. It's . . . but please don't think of me. I'm sure I shall manage.

BERTHA You need someone to keep an eye on you. A housekeeper isn't the same thing.

CHARLES *(unhappily)* No, she isn't, of course.

BERTHA Need someone to look after you properly. You men are so helpless. Who'll nurse you when you're ill? I've known so-called housekeepers who wouldn't even darn a sock or sew on a button.

CHARLES *(looking down at his jacket, from which the button is still missing)* Oh dear. Wouldn't they really?

BERTHA Well, I'll have to think about it. I don't promise.

CHARLES No, don't. I mean, I do think you ought to consider it very carefully. I should hate you to . . .

*(*MAUD *enters R. carrying some knitting.)*

MAUD Has any one seen Emma anywhere? Good morning, Bertha. Have you seen Emma? Oh, Charles, good morning. I was really looking for Emma.

CHARLES As a matter of fact, it was Emma I came to see myself. Is she about anywhere?

ELIZABETH I haven't seen her since breakfast. What do you want her for, Mother? Is it urgent?

MAUD Of course it's urgent. I've dropped a stitch.

ELIZABETH *(rising and crossing to* MAUD*)* Well, give it to me and let me have a look.

MAUD No, you always leave a hole. Emma knows how to do it. Where is she?

ELIZABETH I told you, I haven't seen her since breakfast. As a matter of fact, she seemed rather upset about something—a letter she was reading, I think. I'll go and see where she is and then, if everybody'll excuse me, I must get on. I've wasted half the morning as it is. Shall I tell Emma you want to see her too, Charles?

CHARLES Yes, tell her I've a proposition to make to her.

*(*ELIZABETH *goes out R.)*

MAUD *(sitting R.)* A proposal to Emma, Charles?

CHARLES *(crossing behind* BERTHA'S *chair to R.)* Not—er—exactly a proposal. A proposition. I've heard of a job which I thought might suit her.

MAUD A job? A post for Emma? Does she want one?

CHARLES Well, I rather thought she would be wanting one. Am

I wrong? I understood . . .

MAUD But I thought she was waiting to go back to this old Mrs. Robertson.

CHARLES Robinson . . . Yes, I know she hoped there was that possibility, but . . .

MAUD Oh dear, she can't possibly think of going away yet, anyway.

CHARLES Why not?

MAUD She's the only one who understands the pattern. Elizabeth is quite stupid about it.

CHARLES I'm afraid I don't quite understand.

MAUD My knitting. Emma started it, after all. She can't leave me in the lurch like that.

BERTHA Don't talk to *me* about being left in the lurch.

MAUD I wasn't, dear. I was talking to Charles.

BERTHA I know, and I haven't been able to get a word in. Have you heard the news?

CHARLES Don't you think, Aunt Bertha, that we'd better wait for Sally to tell her grandmother herself?

BERTHA Why? She's bound to know sooner or later.

MAUD What's Sally been doing? I hope she hasn't been a nuisance, Bertha.

BERTHA Oh, I've no quarrel with Sally. I'm rather surprised at Timothy, that's all. He's upset my plans.

MAUD Timothy has? How?

BERTHA He's proposing to get married.

MAUD *(without much interest, as she examines her knitting)* Oh, really? Who to?

BERTHA *(patiently)* To your granddaughter. To Sally.

MAUD *(dropping the knitting in her lap)* To Sally? Did you say he was going to *marry* Sally?

BERTHA That's what I said.

MAUD But that's ridiculous. I can't possibly allow such a thing.

BERTHA *You* can't possibly allow it? I like that. What about me?

MAUD It's nothing to do with you, Bertha. Timothy can do what he likes as far as I'm concerned, but Sally's much to young to get married. What is the child thinking of?

CHARLES Well, apparently she's thinking of getting married. And, if I may say so, she's not as young as all that. I believe she's twenty-one.

MAUD That has nothing to do with it.

CHARLES Oh, sorry. I thought you said it had.

MAUD In any case, I don't think Timothy's at all suitable for her.

BERTHA *(rising menacingly)* Oh, indeed? And why not, pray?

MAUD Because I don't. I hoped, when Sally was old enough to get married, she'd marry somebody—well, somebody rather nice.

BERTHA Well, really! Are you suggesting that my son *isn't* rather nice?

MAUD Of course not, Bertha. I can't think why you should think I meant anything of the sort. I'm very fond of Timothy.

BERTHA But apparently he isn't good enough for your grand-daughter. I never heard such damn cheek in my life. If you're going to make difficulties, Maud . . .

MAUD I'm not making difficulties. I merely said . . .

BERTHA Never see any point of view but your own. It doesn't occur to you to think of *Timothy's* happiness. That's what *I've* got to think of. Mind you, I don't think Sally's good enough for him, but . . .

MAUD Bertha, how dare you say such a thing? My granddaughter not good enough for a twopenny-ha'penny schoolmaster . . .

BERTHA *What's* that?

MAUD *(slightly flustered)* A twopenny-ha'penny schoolmaster? Well, it's . . .

BERTHA Meaning Timothy?

CHARLES Aunt Bertha, please . . .

BERTHA I've had enough. I'm going home. Of all selfish, self-centred women, Maud, you're the worst. And if that's how you feel about me and my family, I think the arrangement about my coming to live here had better be given up.

MAUD *(returning to her examination of the knitting)* Just as you like, dear. I can't think what you'll do, but that's your own affair.

BERTHA *(stumping towards the french window)* You needn't worry. I shall go where I'm appreciated. I shall go with Charles.

CHARLES *(alarmed, and following* BERTHA *to the window)* Oh, Aunt Bertha, please . . .!

*(*BERTHA *storms out through the french window, and at the same time* EMMA, *looking distressed, enters R.)*

EMMA *(coming C.)* Elizabeth said you wanted to see me. I'm sorry I wasn't here.

MAUD Oh, Emma, there you are. I've dropped a stitch.

EMMA *(vaguely)* Dropped what? Oh, yes, a stitch. Yes, of course. *(She takes the knitting, sits in the chair C. and blows her nose.)*

CHARLES *(moving to her)* Is—anything the matter?

EMMA The matter? Oh, no, not really . . . at least . . . I've had some rather sad news, that's all.

CHARLES I'm sorry. Can I . . . is there anything I can do to help?

EMMA *(busy with the knitting)* I'm afraid not, thank you. You see, she's dead.

CHARLES Who?

EMMA Mrs. Robinson. I had a letter from her solicitors this morning—it was forwarded to me from the bank address I gave them. She . . she died quite suddenly, a few days after I left.

CHARLES I'm so very sorry.

EMMA I feel awful—as if I'd deserted her when she needed me most.

CHARLES *(sitting on the arm of her chair)* But you didn't, you know.
It wasn't your fault in any way. I'm sure she knew that.

EMMA Yes . . . Yes, I think she did. But you see, I wish any way
they'd let me know sooner. She died over a fortnight ago.

CHARLES Yes, of course, but . . but you couldn't have done anything
if you had known sooner. You say she died quite suddenly.

EMMA Yes . . . Oh, yes. It isn't that.

CHARLES *(gently)* What is it?

EMMA It's just that . . . after all these years . . . I wish at least I
could have . . . I mean, she'll think it so *strange* of me not even
to have sent a wreath!

*(SALLY enters through the french window. CHARLES rises and
moves L.)*

SALLY *(rushing R. to MAUD)* Oh, there you are, Gran. I say, I
must tell you . . . *(She notices EMMA, and turns to her)* Emma,
darling, is anything the matter?

CHARLES She's had some rather bad news. Don't worry her . . .
I'm afraid I must go. Let me know if I can do anything.

EMMA Didn't you want to see me about something?

CHARLES Did I?

EMMA I understood Elizabeth to say you wanted to speak to me.
But perhaps I was mistaken.

CHARLES Oh, no, if Elizabeth said so I'm sure she was right, but I
confess that for the life of me I can't think what it was . . . Any
way, I won't bother you any more now. Goodbye for the
present. *(He goes towards the french window, and pauses thoughtfully)* Now, what could it have been? *(He looks again at
EMMA in a puzzled way, shakes his head, and goes out through the
window.)*

SALLY Emma, what . . . Oh, all right, I won't bother you.

EMMA You're not bothering me. I must cheer up and stop bothering other people . . . There, I think that's all right now. *(She
hands the knitting to MAUD)* It's only poor old Mrs. Robinson,
Sally.

SALLY Oh, have you heard from her?

EMMA Well, not from *her* exactly. She died about a fortnight
ago.

SALLY *(kneeling beside EMMA's chair)* Oh, Emma! I say, I *am*
sorry. And now there's no chance of your going back to her.
What a shame. What will you do?

EMMA I hadn't thought of it like that, yet. But of course I shall
have to now.

(SALLY sits back on her heels at EMMA's feet, and looks thoughtful.)

SALLY Emma . . .

EMMA Yes?

SALLY I suppose you hadn't thought of it like this, either, but did
she . . . I mean, I wonder if she left you any money after all.

EMMA *(after a pause)* Yes, as a matter of fact, she did.

SALLY Oh, good. That's something to be thankful for, any way.
One in the eye for that old cat of a daughter! Did she leave you
enough?

EMMA Enough?

SALLY Well, something worth having, I mean.

EMMA She has left me—an annuity. That's really what the
solicitor's letter was about. Quite an adequate annuity, as a
matter of fact.

SALLY Enough to live on?

EMMA Yes . . . Yes, I think it would be enough for me to live on,
if I was careful.

SALLY Oh, good! So you needn't think about another job after
all. You can find a nice little cottage, or a bed-sit. or something,
and settle down with a cat.

EMMA *(without enthusiasm)* Thank you, dear.

SALLY What's the matter? Aren't you pleased about the money?

EMMA Oh, yes, very pleased. It was very generous of poor Mrs.
Robinson. But . . .

SALLY But what?

EMMA I don't think I shall like settling down by myself—not even
with a cat.

SALLY *(rising and going behind* EMMA's *chair, to sit on sofa L.)* Oh,
I see. No, it might be a bit lonely. What you really need is a
husband. I wish I could think of a nice widower, or an Elderly
Bachelor of Good Character.

EMMA No, thank you, dear. I don't think I could be bothered
with him at my time of life.

SALLY You're not as old as all that, are you? Nothing like as
old as Gran, for instance. You won't be really old for years yet.

EMMA No, I hope I shan't. That's just it. I don't want to start
living just for myself yet. You see, I've always had someone to
look after, someone rather dependent on me. First it was my own
mother, then Mrs. Robinson. When I was much younger, I
found it rather irksome sometimes; but now I suppose it's become
a habit. Like drugs or drink or something.

SALLY I see. You mean, even though you don't have to, you'd
rather go on being a companion or something. How funny.

EMMA *(apologetically)* Yes, it is rather. I think I must be a little
odd—some people are . . . However, that's quite enough about
me. When you came in just now you said you had something
to tell your grandmother, and I'm afraid we started talking about
my affairs instead. I'm so sorry.

SALLY Oh, that's all right. I was only going to tell her I've got
engaged.

EMMA Engaged? My dear, how lovely. Is it . . . ?

SALLY Yes, Timothy, of *course*. Isn't it marvellous? Gran,
you're not listening. Did you hear what I said?

MAUD *(knitting)* What did you say, dear?

SALLY   Well, I'm bothered. She didn't even hear. Gran, darling,
I'm trying to tell you I'm engaged to Timothy. Timothy—and—
I—*(slowly and deliberately)* are—going—to—be—*married.*

MAUD *(indifferently)* Married? Oh, yes, Bertha said something
about it . . . Emma, I was just thinking about what you said just
now . . .

*(*TOM *enters R. and comes to L. of* MAUD'S *chair.)*

SALLY   Grandpa! I've got engaged!

TOM   Got what? Oh, yes, I know. I say, Maudie . . .

SALLY   How do you know?

TOM   Because somebody told me—Timothy or someone. I say,
Maud, I've had an idea.

*(*CHARLES *enters by the french window.)*

SALLY   Charles! Isn't it thrilling? I'm engaged.

CHARLES   Yes, so I hear. Good . . . *(To* EMMA*)* I'm so sorry to
barge in, but I've just remembered what it was I came about before,
and in the circumstances I thought perhaps . . .

*(*ELIZABETH *enters R.)*

SALLY   Oh, there's Aunt Liz. I say, Aunt Liz . . .

ELIZABETH *(coming behind* EMMA'S *chair)* Has any one got the right
time? My watch has stopped, and the kitchen clock's bust.

SALLY   I shall bust in a minute. Why won't any one *listen?*

TOM   I wish someone would listen to *me* a minute.

CHARLES   I'm afraid I'm butting in rather. Perhaps I'd better . . .

MAUD   You know, I've been thinking . . .

TOM   ⎫
SALLY ⎬ *(together)* Oh, do *listen!*

(A sudden silence.)

CHARLES   I'll come back later. *(He goes out through the french
window.)*

ELIZABETH *(moving to sofa L. and sitting on the arm)* What are
you all making such a song about?

MAUD   I simply can't imagine. I started to say something to Emma
about ten minutes ago, and then everyone started talking, and I
haven't been able to get a word in. And I've had an idea.

TOM   No, you haven't, it was my idea. I came in on purpose to
tell you, but nobody takes any interest.

SALLY   No, they don't.

ELIZABETH   Well, why don't you try one at a time?

TOM   That's what *I* say. Now, listen, Maudie, then *you* can talk.
I've been talking to Whatsisname . . .

SALLY   Who's Whatsisname?

TOM   Don't interrupt. You know who I mean—your young
man . . . .

SALLY   Timothy? Oh, then . . .

TOM   Don't *interrupt.* Yes, Timothy. Well, he says he's getting
married.

SALLY *(with an exasperated sigh)* That's what I've been trying to tell you.

TOM Nonsense. He told me himself. So I said "In that case you'll want somewhere to live." I thought of that at once.

MAUD *(impatiently)* I see. Well, now listen to my idea.

TOM I haven't finished yet. "You'll want somewhere to live," I said. "A flat or a house or something." And then I had my idea.

MAUD Do get on, Tom. What idea?

TOM I'm telling you. "Now, houses are difficult to get," I said. "Can't *get* a house round here." And it seems he wants to live near here for some reason. Can't remember why. New job or something.

MAUD Come to the point, Tom.

TOM I'm *coming* to the point. Give me time. Now, the thing is, I suddenly thought about the top floor.

MAUD What top floor?

TOM Our top floor, of course. Whose top floor would I mean? Now, you know, I once suggested it could be made into a flat?

MAUD *I* said it could be made into a flat for Bertha, but you wouldn't agree.

TOM No, no, not for Bertha. For Whatsisname and Sally. As I said when I suggested it before, it practically *is* a flat already. It's even got a bathroom and a thingummybob.

ELIZABETH Do you mean a kitchen?

TOM Of course I don't mean a kitchen. You don't have a kitchen on the top floor.

ELIZABETH You do if it's meant to be a flat.

TOM Well, we can shove in a sink or whatever you have, if necessary.

ELIZABETH It would be necessary. And a cooker.

TOM *(crossing to L. and standing behind SALLY)* I haven't had time to think of *extras* yet . . . But jolly good idea, eh?

SALLY *(kneeling up on the sofa and hugging TOM over the back of it)* It's a marvellous idea, Grandpa. Thank you a million times. You *are* clever.

TOM *(modestly)* Oh, I don't know . . . What do you think, Maudie?

MAUD Very nice, dear, when Sally grows up and gets married. We shall have to see. *I'm* thinking of something which affects us *now*.

SALLY But, Grannie . . .

MAUD Don't interrupt, dear, Grannie's talking. I was thinking about Emma.

EMMA Oh, please don't worry about me.

MAUD I wasn't worrying, I was thinking. And I think, as you haven't got to go back to Mrs. Robertson now, you might as well stay here for good.

EMMA Oh, but . . .

MAUD Of course, if you don't want to, there's no more to be said.

EMMA *(distressed)* Oh, please . . . It isn't that. I should love to,
but . . .

MAUD But what? You said you didn't want to live alone.

EMMA No, I don't. Indeed I don't. But you don't need me—
I should be just in the way. You've got Elizabeth to . . .

MAUD *(haughtily)* I fail to see what it has to do with Elizabeth.

EMMA *(nearly crying with confusion)* But of course it has . . . I . . . .
(turning to ELIZABETH*)* Elizabeth, please don't think I . . . Oh,
dear, how difficult it all is . . . *(pleadingly)* Elizabeth . . .

ELIZABETH *(rising and putting her arm round* EMMA's *shoulder)* It's
all *right*, Emma. *(She straightens up and faces* MAUD*)* Mother,
are you suggesting that Emma should stay here for good—make
her home here?

MAUD Of course. That's what I said. And I don't quite see
why *you* should object.

ELIZABETH *(very quietly)* I'm not objecting, you know.

MAUD In any case, I thought you said not long ago that you wanted
to go away from home. If Emma was here, there wouldn't be
any particular need for you to stay if you didn't want to.

EMMA *(rising and facing* ELIZABETH*) Did* you say that, Elizabeth?

ELIZABETH Yes, I did say so.

EMMA *(eagerly)* And if I stay, you might be able to . . . to . . . I
mean, I shan't be just in the way?

ELIZABETH Would you really like to stay—whether I'm here or not.

EMMA More than anything in the world.

ELIZABETH *(slowly and with great feeling)* Then—I should like you
to stay . . . more than anything in the world.
*(*ELIZABETH *turns and goes out quickly R.)*

MAUD Well, that's settled, then; and now there's no hurry about
my knitting, so I think I shall leave it and go for a walk in the
garden. *(She begins to wind up the knitting, then stops to examine
it)* Oh dear, I've dropped another stitch.

EMMA I'll pick it up for you while you're out. *(*EMMA *takes the
knitting and helps* MAUD *to her feet)* It's lovely outside. You'll
both enjoy a little walk.

MAUD Yes, I think we shall. Come along, Tom.

TOM Come along where?

MAUD You heard what Emma said. She thinks a walk would do
us good.

TOM Oh, does she? All right, good idea.

MAUD Now, I wonder if I ought to have my coat.

EMMA I'll get it for you if think you'll need it; but I really think
you'll find it too much. It's very warm. What do you think?

MAUD *(considering)* Yes, perhaps I shall. All right.

EMMA In fact I should go at once, before the sun gets *too* hot.

MAUD *(almost meekly, as she goes towards the window)* Yes, Emma.
*(*MAUD *goes out through the french window.* TOM *starts to follow
her, then pauses and turns back.)*

TOM *(to* EMMA*)* Did somebody say you were going to stay here for good?

EMMA *(smiling)* I hope so.

TOM Oh, good. *(Patting her on the arm.)* You know, I *like* you . . . Don't like everybody . . . Don't like Bertha . . . *(Still muttering, he potters out through the french window.* EMMA *sits C. and begins to pick up the stitch in the knitting.)*

SALLY *(lying back on the sofa with a deep sigh of bliss)* Isn't it heavenly?

*(*TIMOTHY *enters R.)*

TIMOTHY What's heavenly?

SALLY Life . . . Emma's going to stay here for ever, and we're going to be married, and Grandpa's going to put in a sink on the top floor for us, and—and I don't think I've got a thing left to wish for.

EMMA *(rolling up the knitting and rising)* Yes, it's all lovely; and, do you know, I haven't even congratulated you both yet. *(She goes to* SALLY *and kisses her)* My dear, I'm so glad, you know that. *(Holding out her hand to* TIMOTHY*)* And I think you're very lucky.

TIMOTHY Thank you, Emma darling, I know I am. *(He puts his arms round* EMMA *and gives her a hearty kiss.)*

EMMA *(overcome)* Oh, *Wilfred!* *(She backs away from him)* Oh dear, I've just realised—you might have been . . . I mean I might have been your . . . Well, any way, *(recovering herself)* if I'm going to stay here, and you're going to have the top floor, I can think of *another* way I might be of use by and by.

SALLY How?

EMMA Baby-sitting.

*(*EMMA *is again overcome with confusion as she realises where her thoughts have led her, and goes out hurriedly R.)*

SALLY Isn't she a lamb?

TIMOTHY *(sitting beside her)* She's a darling, and so are you. Happy? *(He takes her in his arms.)*

SALLY I'm so happy that it *hurts* . . . *(She looks thoughtful)* Darling . . .

TIMOTHY Yes, darling?

SALLY *(her head on his shoulder)* You know Grandpa says we can have the top floor?

TIMOTHY Yes. Jolly good of him. You'll like that, won't you?

SALLY Oh, I shall love it. It's just that I was wondering . . .

TIMOTHY *(tenderly)* What, my pet?

SALLY Oh, nothing, really. It's silly to mind.

TIMOTHY Tell me what's worrying you.

SALLY *(hesitating)* Well, he's going to put in a cooker and a sink. Do you think *(with a sudden rush)* he'll run to one of those nice stainless steel ones?

*(*TIMOTHY, *overcome with emotion at these beautiful words, kisses*

57

her again, as ELIZABETH *comes in R. with an old basket in her hand.)*

ELIZABETH Oh, not *again?* Can't you go and do that in the summer house, or somewhere out of the way?

TIMOTHY *(with great dignity, as he releases* SALLY *and they both rise)* As a matter of fact, we were having a most important discussion on the subject of kitchen sinks.

ELIZABETH *(coming C.)* Oh? Oh, well we all have our own way of doing things . . . By the way, Sally, as everyone else seems to know about you two, I suppose you've told your mother?

TIMOTHY *(with feeling)* I have. You told me to.

ELIZABETH Good. I hope you did it nicely.

TIMOTHY Well . . . I asked her permission, of course, to—er—pay my addresses to her daughter . . .

ELIZABETH That was a fat lot of good, when you've already been paying them all over the place. What did she say?

TIMOTHY *(hesitating)* She . . . Oh, well, any way, we talked her round.

ELIZABETH Oh, did she need talking round? What was her objection?

TIMOTHY Only that—well—Sally was a bit young, and I was a bit old, and so forth. We pointed out that I'd still got most of my hair and might be expected to live a few years longer, and that Sally was of age, and . . . *(PRUDENCE enters through the french window)* Well, well, here's Mother-in-law herself. *(PRUDENCE glares.)*

SALLY *(going towards the door R. and* TIMOTHY *following)* As a matter of fact, I think what really worries her is that she doesn't fancy herself as a potential grandmother. *(To* PRUDENCE, *with a pert smile)* Do you, darling?

*(*TIMOTHY *and* SALLY *go out laughing R.)*

PRUDENCE *(sitting L.)* You seem to have more time than usual to stand about gossiping this morning. I thought you were always so busy.

ELIZABETH *(perching on arm of chair C.)* I am. I was just on my way to the garden to find some veg. for lunch. But I'm a bit demoralised this morning, what with one thing and another. Well, what do you think of the news?

PRUDENCE Which particular bit of news do you mean?

ELIZABETH Well, Heavens above! Sally and Timothy, of course. What did you think I meant?

PRUDENCE Oh, that. Well, I suppose Sally's old enough to please herself—at least, so she tells me. I thought perhaps you meant about Emma.

ELIZABETH *(rising and going thoughtfully to the french window)* Oh, you know about that already, do you?

PRUDENCE I met Mamma, and she was full of it. I suppose it's all right. Pity they didn't think of it before. It might have solved your problems.

ELIZABETH *(turning)* Might have?

PRUDENCE I thought you said you wanted someone to come and cope with the parents, instead of you.

ELIZABETH So I did. So I do.

PRUDENCE Do? But I thought it was because you had this idea of getting married.

ELIZABETH That was one of the reasons—the chief reason, in fact. What about it?

PRUDENCE Only that it's a bit late, isn't it, since he's apparently changed his mind.

ELIZABETH *(coming down to R. of the sofa)* Who's changed his mind? What are you talking about? What makes you think anybody's changed his mind?

PRUDENCE Well, damn it all, considering the man's now engaged to my own daughter . . .

(ELIZABETH looks at PRUDENCE in bewildered silence for several seconds, then turns, moves to behind chair C. and faces her again.)

ELIZABETH *(slowly)* Do you mean . . You didn't think I meant Timothy, did you? Not *Timothy?*

PRUDENCE Of course I thought you meant Timothy? Who else?

ELIZABETH *(recovering from her surprise and beginning to smile)* Who else, indeed? Well, well. What on earth did I say to make you think that? I'm quite certain I never told you that Timothy had even . . . I mean, I simply can't think what gave you that idea.

PRUDENCE You told me distinctly that you had had what you so quaintly described as an Offer, which you were dying to accept.

ELIZABETH Yes, but . . . not *Timothy's* offer . . . I—I mean, I didn't say anything about Timothy.

PRUDENCE Yes, you did. In almost the same breath you said something about discussing things with Timothy, and that it was he who had suggested that I should come here and relieve you of the parents.

ELIZABETH Oh, I see. Yes, I believe that *was* his idea. Not a very good one, actually. But any way, that was another . . . on another occasion.

PRUDENCE Naturally, I put two and two together.

ELIZABETH *(turning and going towards the window)* And made about five or six at least . . . Oh dear, how funny. *(She starts to laugh.)*

PRUDENCE I don't see that it's funny.

ELIZABETH *(over her shoulder)* No, you wouldn't. But it is.

ELIZABETH *goes out, still laughing, through the french window.* PRUDENCE *rises, makes as if to follow her, hesitates, then goes to the cigarette box U.L. and takes a cigarette. She comes down thoughtfully C. as she lights it.* CHARLES *enters R.)*

CHARLES Oh, hello, Prudence. Sorry to disturb you, but Florrie said she thought Elizabeth was in here.

PRUDENCE She's just gone into the garden. I don't suppose she'll be long. *(She sits C.)*

CHARLES *(coming down R.)* Well, really, I ought not to stay. It's just something I meant to mention when I came before. I seem to have been popping in and out of this house for the last hour. I keep forgetting things this morning—can't think why. It must be all this excitement. I say, I'm jolly glad about Timothy and Sally. Good show, don't you think?

PRUDENCE Yes . . . Yes, it is, of course.

CHARLES *(anxiously)* Aren't you pleased about it? I mean, I know Timothy is my cousin, and all that, but I don't think I'm prejudiced.

PRUDENCE Oh, I've nothing against Timothy. I'm thinking of Sally herself. She's so *young*, Charles—like I was. I don't want her to make the mistake I made.

CHARLES I don't think you need worry about Sally. She's got her head screwed on all right . . I mean . . . well, er . . . *(He flounders, and decides to change the subject)* I expect you'll miss her a bit, of course.

PRUDENCE *(sadly)* Yes, I'm afraid I was thinking of myself a little, too. One tries not to be selfish, but . . well . . . Sally's all I have now. All I ever had, really. I'm rather a lonely sort of person, you know, Charles, and I've never had anyone who — who *understood* me. Do you know what I mean?

CHARLES Yes, I think I see what you're driving at, but . . .

PRUDENCE *(looking up at him)* I think *you* are rather an understanding person, Charles.

CHARLES Oh . . . well . . . er . . . it's rather my job to . . .er . . .

PRUDENCE *(intensely)* Do *you* know what it's like to be lonely?

CHARLES *(very quietly)* Yes.

PRUDENCE *(sharply)* What did you say?

CHARLES I said, yes, I do.

PRUDENCE Oh . . . Well, then . . . *(Getting into her stride again)* I suppose you think I'm a happy sort of woman. I don't show my feelings to the world. I'm calm and composed, and outwardly perhaps even a little hard sometimes. But it's all a pose. Somewhere underneath that calm and composed exterior there's a heart, Charles. A heart longing for real affection and . . .

CHARLES I say, Prudence, are you all right?

PRUDENCE What do you mean? I'm trying to tell you—to show you what I'm . . .

CHARLES Yes, I know, but you don't usually go on like this. Have you been out in the sun or something? It's awfully hot.

PRUDENCE *(rising and making a last effort)* Charles! *(She lays a gentle hand on his arm, and tries to look into his eyes.)*

CHARLES *(frightened but firm)* Look here, Prudence, I think I'd better go and find Elizabeth. I'm rather in a hurry.

(CHARLES rushes through the french window, just as TIMOTHY and

SALLY *enter R.)*

SALLY *(rushing towards the window)* Oh, there he is! I say, Charles . . . *(But* CHARLES *has gone)* Oh, bother, Florrie said he was here, and I wanted to ask him something. Why is he in such a hurry? *(She looks at* PRUDENCE, *who is angrily attending to her face)* Mummie! You haven't been trying that game on Charles, have you? Not Charles, of all people?

PRUDENCE What on earth are you talking about?

SALLY Darling, really, there are limits. I mean—a *parson!* It's sacrilege!
*(*PRUDENCE, *beside herself with rage, opens her mouth to say something, changes her mind, and goes out R., slamming the door.)*

TIMOTHY Good Lord, do you think she'd been trying to get off with Charles?

SALLY *(moving L. and sitting on the sofa)* I don't know, but it did look rather like it. Poor old Charles, you'd think he of all people might be safe.

TIMOTHY Oh, Charles can take care of himself. He's done it for a good many years.

SALLY *(thoughtfully)* Yes.

TIMOTHY Now what's biting you?

SALLY Nothing. I've just had rather an idea, that's all. I don't suppose he would, though.

TIMOTHY *(coming towards her)* Everybody's full of ideas this morning. And I've got another.

SALLY What is it?

TIMOTHY *(pulling her to her feet)* This . . . *(He embraces her)* I've had that idea before, I know, and I shall probably have it again. *(He does.)*

SALLY *(in his arms)* Darling . . .

TIMOTHY Yes, darling?

SALLY Nothing darling. I was just thinking.

TIMOTHY About me, I hope.

SALLY Partly. And partly about Aunt Liz.

TIMOTHY Oh-ho! Jealous?

SALLY No. I was just thinking what a lot she's missed.

TIMOTHY Meaning me?

SALLY No, not you particularly. Just generally. Poor Aunt Liz!
(They kiss again, as ELIZABETH *enters through the french window, with her basket full of vegetables. She gives an exasperated sigh, puts down the basket, and goes and takes* SALLY *and* TIMOTHY *by the arm.)*

ELIZABETH *(pushing them towards the door R.)* Out!

TIMOTHY Just as you say—*Auntie!*
*(*TIMOTHY *and* SALLY *go out R.* ELIZABETH *shuts the door after them, then crosses to her workbasket on the table U.L. and gets a needle and thread.)*

ELIZABETH *(calling towards the french window)* Where are you?

Come on in, and I'll do it now.

(CHARLES *appears at the window, fingering the place where the missing button ought to be.*)

CHARLES Honestly, it doesn't matter. Don't bother now. It's been off for weeks, any way.

ELIZABETH I know, and I can't bear it any longer. I suppose you haven't got the button?

CHARLES *(coming down C.)* Yes, I have, as a matter of fact—I think. *(He fumbles in his pockets)* I know I kept it carefully. Ah, here it is . . . *(He brings out a large button, and looks at it)* No, it isn't, that's the one which came off my mackintosh. *(He feels again, and brings out a smaller button)* Yes, that's it. But really, you know . . .

ELIZABETH *(seizing the button)* You needn't take it off. Stand still a minute.

(She begins to sew the button on, while CHARLES *looks down at her. He puts his hand gently on hers, and she stops sewing and looks up. Then with* ELIZABETH *holding the needle and thread rather dangerously at arm's length,* CHARLES *puts his arms round her and kisses her. They do not hear the door R. open as* EMMA *enters.)*

EMMA *(in maidenly confusion)* Oh! I'm so sorry! *(She goes out hurriedly R., then almost immediately opens the door and comes in again, her expression changed to one of smiling approval)* I mean —I'm so, *so* glad!

CURTAIN.

PRODUCTION NOTES

The set should represent a bright, pleasant, comfortable room, with chintz-covered chairs, and furniture which looks " good." It is neither a modern " lounge " nor an overcrowded Victorian parlour, but the old-type drawing-room of an elderly couple. On a small stage the furniture should be kept to the minimum shown in the plot and if necessary a third armchair can be used instead of the sofa. To save space, cigarette-box, magazines, etc. are found on the top of the book-case; but if there is room, or if the book-case is of unsuitable height, an extra small table may be used for these. As the season is high summer, the french windows can remain open throughout, with a backcloth showing the garden.

This is mainly a " light-hearted " comedy, and the general pace must be quick and lively, and the dialogue kept going, with as much legitimate movement and business as possible to prevent conversations becoming static. If this is remembered, the occasional pauses, where they are indicated, will add point to the few more serious moments, which should be given their full value: for instance, in Act III, when ELIZABETH suddenly realises what EMMA's making her home with MAUD will mean to her own future. Her line " Then I should like you to stay—more than anything in the world " is said with real feeling, and after her exit there should be a slight pause before MAUD breaks the spell with a fatuous remark about her knitting—and the atmosphere returns to comedy. Again, towards the end of Act III, in the scene between ELIZABETH and PRUDENCE, ELIZABETH's line "Do you mean . . . You didn't think I meant Timothy, did you? " should be preceded by a short, mystified pause and then said very slowly This is the climax of the play, and the audience, as well as PRUDENCE, must have time to adjust its ideas.

Most of the characters can be taken at their face-value. MAUD is completely selfish but not vicious—she is merely so incredibly stupid that she simply doesn't realise her own selfishness. TOM, on the other hand, rather enjoys his own reputation for eccentricity and plays up to it, though he should avoid overdoing it and becoming a clown. BERTHA and FLORRIE speak for themselves (in every way!) and TIMOTHY is an ordinary "nice" young man, in some ways a little immature for thirty-four. PRUDENCE is very well-dressed, very sophisticated, and, like MAUD, completely selfish, but in a more calculating way. She is languid in speech and movement, and utterly feline.

ELIZABETH is *not* a conventional " Cinderella " either in appearance or character. Though a complete contrast to PRUDENCE, she can be both good-looking and well-dressed in a quieter way, and even in an apron should look neat and attractive, and not a careworn hag. She is completely human, with a lot of common sense, a down-to-earth attitude to life, and a sense of humour which is often tried to the point of making the occasional acid remark. In Act II she shows signs of irritation and strain after a particularly trying day and this culminates in her outburst to MAUD at the end of the act.

EMMA needs care. Superficially she is insignificant and a little dowdy, but not grotesquely so, and she is certainly not a figure of fun. She is capable of real feeling, and should show it when necessary, in a restrained way—when she is listening to the letter at the end of Act I, and in Act II when she is telling SALLY of her engagement to TIMOTHY's father, and (momentarily) when TOM unconsciously puts his foot in it about her one-time fiancé. One may laugh at EMMA a little, but with affection, and should end by respecting her—like the nicest kind of maiden aunt.

SALLY is very vivacious, rather young for her age in some ways, but with an underlying shrewdness. Unlike some of her contemporaries, she does not take either life in general or herself in particular too seriously, but she sums up her own character when she says " Beneath a youthful and frivolous exterior I have great perspicacity . . ."

CHARLES should not look or behave like either the stage "comic" parson or the over-hearty type. He is just a " good sort "—sincere, human, and lovable —and if he can be reasonably tall and handsome as well, all the better! By the final curtain the audience should have grown to like him well enough to feel satisfied and happy about his marrying ELIZABETH—not that she is merely " making the best of a bad job " at the advanced age of thirty-eight.

Dress presents no difficulties, as all the characters wear the ordinary summer clothes of people of their respective ages and types. Remember that in Act II they should *not* be in evening dress. The guests have stayed on to a late supper after a cocktail party, and are still attired in whatever they would have been wearing for that party—the men in lounge suits, PRUDENCE and possibly SALLY in " cocktail dresses," and the other women in the ordinary afternoon dresses which they probably would wear for such occasions in a quiet country place.

FURNITURE

Armchair: At angle R.

Armchair: C.

Sofa: At angle L.

Small table: At angle across corner U.L.

Standard lamp: L. of french window.

Bookcase, filled with books, against wall R. of french window. *On it:* Magazines, cigarette box (with cigarettes) ash-tray, matches.

Cushions on armchairs and sofa.

Pictures, additional small chairs or tables (optional, and only if there is room without overcrowding.)

PROPERTIES
ACT I
On stage

Pile of parcels (including one roughly the size and shape of a cricket bat) on table U.L.

Vacuum cleaner beside bookcase.

Coat over back of chair C.

Two books on chair R.

Off stage

Greetings telegram envelope (FLORRIE).

Pencil (ELIZABETH).

Laundry book (ELIZABETH).

Laundry basket with crumpled linen, including: 3 sheets, 3 bath towels, 6 table napkins, 1 pr. pyjamas, 1 afternoon teacloth, and 1 very dirty roller towel (ELIZABETH).

Personal

Duster (ELIZABETH)

Packet of cigarettes and matches (FLORRIE).

Shopping basket with parcels (BERTHA).

Handbag (BERTHA).

Shopping list (BERTHA).

Cigarette lighter (TIMOTHY).

Handbag containing powder compact, etc. (PRUDENCE).

Pipe, tobacco pouch, matches (TOM).

Small change (TOM).

2 letters, stamped and addressed and already opened—one written out in full, to be read aloud by Maud (CHARLES).

Diary (CHARLES).

Jacket with one button missing (CHARLES).

ACT II
On stage

Several cocktail glasses, some with dregs in the bottom, on table, bookcase, etc.

Plate, with 2 cocktail snacks, on table U.L.

Tray (FLORRIE).

N.B.—*Strike* pile of parcels on table U.L.

Off stage

Tray with coffee, milk, and 4 small coffee cups (FLORRIE).

Personal

Cigarette lighter (TIMOTHY).

Apron (CHARLES).

Pipe and tobacco pouch (CHARLES).

Matches (TOM).

ACT III
On stage

Vase (empty) for flowers, on table U.L.

Workbasket, with needles and thread, on table U.L.

Matches (removed by CHARLES in Act II) replaced on bookcase U.R.

Off stage

Flowers (ELIZABETH).

Old basket or trug (ELIZABETH).

Vegetables (ELIZABETH).

Personal

Cigarette lighter (TIMOTHY).

Duster (FLORRIE).

Knitting (MAUD).

Handkerchief (EMMA).

2 buttons (CHARLES).

Jacket as in Act 1, with button missing (CHARLES).

LIGHTING
ACT I

Daylight—a sunny summer morning.

ACT II

Artificial light—apparently only from one standard lamp at the opening of the act, but with enough light to show FLORRIE'S business with the glasses. Full lighting is switched on by MAUD at her entrance. Moonlight on garden backing.

ACT III

Same as Act I.